To [illegible]
you got it is all [illegible]
Love.

Love
Alejandra [illegible]

GOD IS LOVE

And Hell is Not

ISBN 978-0-9964086-6-0

Published by:
Middle River Press
Oakland Park, Florida
middleriverpress.com.

info@middleriverpress.com

Printed in the U.S.A.

GOD IS LOVE

And Hell is Not

A Message of Love to All

Alejandro O. Tamargo

To Jerry Burke Jr., who taught me that it is the substance of what we do in life that is really important.

God is Love, and Hell is not;
a message of Love to All

When we choose love we are choosing God

Introduction and Background for this Book

Whether you believe in God or not, it should be self-evident to everyone, just by your own personal experiences, that where there is no love, there is much of what most of us think is in hell: misery, anger, hate, greed, and unhappiness. So the opposite of love is really hell. Just like the opposite of light is darkness.

In my church we pray for peace on earth to men of goodwill, but men of goodwill have chosen to have goodwill, and they already have peace on earth within them and around them; love and goodwill are choices all of us can, and should, make to have peace and happiness in our lives. What believers should really focus on, in their prayers to God, is for God to help everyone to get, and always maintain, goodwill and love all of the time. No matter what any of our brothers and sisters do, or don't do, God will help all of us to choose love. When any one of us decides to have goodwill and love toward others, we are choosing to have peace and love within us and around us. We are called to love because that is what God is, unimaginable love.

"It is by this all men will know you are My disciples, if you have love for one another"(John 13:35). Christians, more than anyone else, should know: **"If you really know me, you will know my Father as well…"**(John 14:7)

God is Love, and Hell is not.

It was at the beginning of 2013 when I started writing these messages as they came to me; most of the time it was in the middle of the night or when I was working out and my mind was open and not cluttered with what was going on around me.

The following is the link for my son Marc's movie; he was going to film school in 2013, and made this short six-minute movie in New Zealand as an entry to a film festival in 2012. Marc asked me to tell him what I thought of it. He asked me to do this after I had already written a good portion of "God is Love, and Hell is not; a message of Love to all," and yet it seemed to fit so well with the theme of what I was in the middle of writing; he called his film "Moving On." What is in this book is about mankind needing to be humble and to know that none of our bowls hold the entire ocean that is God. My son's film shows a girl wading out to the ocean to fetch a suitcase containing baggage she no longer needed, and dumping it on the shore of the ocean, and then being able to move on with her life. In the message contained in this book you are being asked to get rid of the extra baggage of some of your beliefs that are not serving you well, and keep only the beliefs that will bring you closer to God. This message mentions this coincidence in the hope that it will help you believe you are special, and all of your brothers and sisters in your world are also very special to God.

The movie will only take six minutes of your time, but if you keep your ears and your heart open it might change your world. My son did not mean for his movie to be spiritual because at the time he made the movie he did not believe in God and considered himself agnostic, but yet...

The link to "Moving On":

http://www.youtube.com/watch?v=TAhVJYUx5m4

Starting in 2014 I began reading books with "love" in the theme. I first read *Love is a Choice* by Dr. Robert Hemfelt, Dr. Frank Minirth, and Dr. Paul Meier, and then I read *A Return to Love* by Marianne Williamson. *Love is a Choice* was more about relationships and addictions with some spiritual thoughts thrown in, and *A Return to Love* was more spiritual with some thoughts on relationships thrown in. I have also bought and read an English translation of the Qur'an by M.A.S. Abdel Haleem.

After reading *Love is a Choice* and *A Return to Love*, I can see how the two concepts, relationships and spirituality, are tied together by the love theme. I am looking forward to learning more from what others have written before me, and from some of the thoughts and revelations coming to me directly by asking to be an instrument of God's love. The one thing I am absolutely certain of, as I write this book is that where there is love, there is God. And where there is no love, we are deciding to keep God out; which will always be our choice to make, because God has granted us free will.

The following are some of my impressions that I want to share with you, after my reading of the Qur'an: The Prophet Muhammad must have been inspired by God to write much of what was written in the Qur'an. But, one of the main messages I have received, when praying to be an instrument of God's love is calling me to deliver, is that God loves all of us equally and unconditionally, and therefor God is on all of ours sides; God doesn't just love those who read and believe the Qur'an or just those who read and believe the Bible or any other of mankind's holy books. God loves every one of us unconditionally, no matter what we believe or don't believe, and God has been calling on us to do the same. If you want to truly love God, you have to love all those who are also loved by God. The Prophet Muhammad did say God has been sending us messengers throughout our history, and he did not say he would be the last messenger God would ever send us. However, it should also be self-evident to you by where we are now, that mankind has only a foundation and a beginning in our spiritual journey. **And as a child would ask the question: "Are we there yet?" Your answer should be: "No, we are just starting, but at least no longer completely lost."**

I thought I was almost finished with my writing, and really feeling a sense of urgency due to all the unnecessary harm mankind is still continuing to inflict on one another – in the fall of 2014. Around that time my oldest son – Alejandro who is named after me – father and mother-in law, Jim and Marguerite Kendall, were going to be visiting the Washington area to attend a navy reunion all the surviving crew members of U.S. Navy ship Earle B. Hall APD107 have been holding for the past several years in different cities of the United States; in September of 2014 they were holding their reunion at a hotel right outside of Washington DC in Arlington Virginia. They had called my wife and me and left us a message to let us know they were going to be in our area and would like to stop by and visit us where we live, in Annapolis, Maryland; Arlington Virginia is only an hour's drive to our house. We called them back and asked them to please stay with us – for at least a couple days – while visiting our area. When our oldest son got married in Portland, Oregon, we had stayed at their house for almost a week, and my wife and I were looking forward to the opportunity of trying to match how they had made us feel, very much like we were part of their family when we stayed with them.

While Jim was visiting us I talked to him about some of what I have been writing, and he told me that when he got back to Oregon he was going to mail me a book he had recently read that resonated with many of the things I told him I was writing about. The book Jim thought I would want to read is *Proof of Heaven* by Eben Alexander, MD. I finished reading *Proof of Heaven* on Sunday October 26, 2014. That Sunday when I went to church the Gospel read during the service, Matthew 22:34-40, told us the bottom line of all of God's commandments: "'**You shall love the Lord your God with your whole heart, with your whole soul, and with all your mind.' This is the greatest and first commandment. The second is like it; 'You shall love your neighbor as yourself.' On these two commandments the whole law is based, and the prophets as well.**"

The Gospel reading was reaffirming God's wish for the choices God wants you to make while you live in this world. What Dr. Alexander told us in his book *Proof of Heaven* about his personal encounter with God's unconditional love for all of us also reaffirmed God's wish for us. You will experience God's love in Heaven in a way that is hard to imagine now, but which is very real; you will get to experience this infinite love after you move on from this world and on to your true home with God.

Jim Kendall was right and there is a lot of what Dr. Alexander told us about God in describing his near death experience that is similar to what I have been writing. And it is interesting to note that Dr. Alexander's last name is the same as mine and my oldest son's first name. Alejandro is Spanish for Alexander. Dr. Alexander told us in his book, he is not particularly special. And he is right about not being particularly special – but all of us are brothers and sisters in this world, and very special to God our father – and that makes us all very special indeed.

Two days after I finished reading Dr. Alexander's book *Proof of Heaven,* the following thought came to me early in the morning as I was working out, and I felt I should put it at the very beginning of my writing – so that if you do not read anything else – you read and believe the title of your message: ***God is Love, and Hell is not.*** It is one of the most important parts of the messages God has been trying to give to mankind and that Dr. Alexander felt during his near death experience. Not realizing the truth that God has unimaginable and unconditional love for all of us with no exceptions for who we are or what we do, is allowing mankind to excuse some not very loving acts as atonement to God; when the truth is that you are always welcome to God's home when you choose love no matter what you might have done before, you just have to **"go and sin no more"** (John 8:11). The most important belief we need to have is the same as what Dr. Alexander told us in his book he experienced in his near death experience, and that God's messages boils down to – **we are all loved by God unconditionally!** All are always welcome to his unconditional love, but God will not force anyone to love, so you have to decide to love and then pray for God's help to keep doing it.

Science is coming around to tell us that much of the personal conflicts, and also societal conflicts, are aggravated by people who do not feel loved. Dr. Alexander told us in his book how he had always felt there was some love missing in his life, no matter how much his parents tried to tell him he had been chosen and was loved very much. He only started to feel loved after he came to find out his birth parents gave him up for adoption, not because they did not love him, but because they did. I believe God made him an instrument of his love for us because Dr. Alexander still did not feel completely loved. He also needed to find out what so many of us need to find out. You have been chosen by God and loved unconditionally. However, after his near death experience he does not have the least doubt – **we are all loved by God unconditionally!**

In addition, after I finish reading *Proof of Heaven* I went back to finish reading *A Course in Miracles* by the Foundation for Inner Peace. I had started reading this book in early 2014, but I put it down to read at a later time. I kept reading almost every other page the word "Atonement" , and although I saw much truth in what the book was telling us – it seem to be missing the most powerful and important of the messages God's has been trying to give to us: **We have always been loved unconditionally by God since God created us. No atonement to God will ever be necessary – only to your brothers and sisters**.

However, as I went on to read *A Course in Miracles* I thought to myself: "Maybe I am not totally understanding the word 'Atonement'"; there was much of what the book was telling us that resonated with me, but not that word it used over and over in the book: "Atonement." I went ahead and did a web search and the following is what I got: Definition of ATONEMENT by Merriam-Webster.com/dictionary/atonement

1. obsolete: reconciliation

2. the reconciliation of God and humankind through the sacrificial death of Jesus Christ

3. reparation for an offense or injury: satisfaction

And then I did a web search for the word "lesson": Definition of LESSON by Merriam-Webster.com/dictionary/lesson

Full Definition of LESSON

1. a passage from sacred writings read in a service of worship

2. a piece of instruction

3. a reading or exercise to be studied by a pupil

4. a division of a course of instruction

It came to me as I read the book that if I substituted the word "lesson" for "atonement" every time I encountered it in the book or "God's unconditional love for mankind," then **the substance of the book** had much to teach me. If I had totally stopped reading the book, as I was first inclined to do, I would have missed some very important "lessons" the book had to teach me. Joyce Sweeney, the professional editor who helped me edit this book, also told me: "this movement also wants you to read the word as at-one-ment meaning a unity with God." And this meaning would also not be a contradiction of God's unconditional love. Unity with God would actually be a great description of **"go and sin no more"** (John 8:11). When you choose love, rather than sin, you bring yourself closer to God. However, the book seemed to contradict the very strong and unconditional love from God I was feeling while writing this message and what I later learned from Dr. Alexander's near death experience. By using "atonement" rather than "lesson" or "God's unconditional love for mankind," or "unity with God," the book contradicted much of what the book itself had to teach. I would have missed a great opportunity to expand my own spiritual journey. No atonement to God is needed, only to each other; God loves us unconditionally – if we had to atone to God – the love would have conditions. For if atonement was needed for God to love us, we would then need to take actions because of our sins first, for God to love us; this would then be a condition to receive God's love. This is contradicting that God loves us unconditionally. **I like to humbly ask you to please understand, God is inspiring me to tell you, atonement for our sins is needed, whenever possible, but is really for our own sake – not God's.** By atoning to others for our misdeeds we make it easier to accept and forgive ourselves first, knowing that God loves us unconditionally and will always welcome us back into his embrace. And then we can do our best, to hence forward, forgive others as we would wish others to forgive us. In addition, by our actions, we make it easier for others to forgive us. And so by our atonement to others we are demonstrating and promoting more love in our world. However, God's love will always embrace us; it is up to us to decide to love, and then go and sin no more. In John 12:30 Jesus said, **"This voice was for your benefit, not mine."**

In his near death experience Dr. Alexander saw our real home in Heaven. Heaven has always been our real home and where God wants us to be with Him and His unimaginable love – but will not force us to be. In the messages God has been trying to give mankind throughout history – it is up to each one of us to decide to be with God. **It is by your love for God and for all of your brothers and sisters here on earth that you connect with God and your brothers and sisters – and then after you die you will also be with God in your real home in Heaven.**

I have also read additional books written by authors who have much knowledge and education on the subject of the message in this book, mostly from Christians, who as I read what they have written, it is plain to see that they have much love for others in their hearts.

The following is yet another coincidence: I received an e-mail from Barnes & Noble regarding a book I had ordered on April 22, 2014. It is Pope Francis' new book published in 2014 called *The Church of Mercy*, and it arrived at my home on April 23. I started to read it the evening of April 24, 2014. After reading this book I found many of the same messages in this book, written in a somewhat different manner, because Pope Francis is applying what he is receiving mostly to the Catholic Church, but somehow what he is receiving is not applicable to those who decide not to join this church. I have also quoted Pope Francis as getting the same messages in my introduction to this message, which I started to write last year. However, as I began to read this book which was just published in 2014, I found many more things in common to with the message God wants us to receive through people who are praying to be instruments of God's love.

This book will continue to mention several "coincidences" that I have noticed happened while writing this message, because you need to believe you are special. And that almost everyone else who God has used in the past to send us his messages of love is not any more special than the least of our brothers and sisters. You need to believe the importance of the message. You are loved equally and unconditionally by God, and you are special to God. **There was one special messenger God did send to us; I believe that special messenger was Jesus Christ. But that was only because God wanted us to know the importance of the message which we were not getting, and that we still do not seem to be getting.** God loves all of us so unconditionally with no exception or exclusions that he sent his Son to give us the message. We need to get it – we are the ones who do the excluding with our love – not God. You and I when we are not as universal with our love as God is with His love, are not making the choice God would want us to make. But God created us with the liberty and the dignity to choose love; you have that God-given right to choose love that no one can take away from you.

The one thing that struck me – after reading *The Church of Mercy* – was that one of the very strong messages I have been getting is that mankind will be better served by focusing on the messages from God to us and not on the messengers; yes, even us Christians who believe God sent his son Jesus to show us a better way to be closer to God, need to focus on Christ's message of love. **We need to remember that Jesus' very life and words were for all of us – not just Christians.** Christians were to be those who in Jesus words: **"it is by your love for one another, that everyone will recognize you as my disciples, if you have love for one another"** (John 13:34 – 35). My brothers and sisters, being a Christian is not about calling yourself a Christian, but knowing – no matter how you have come to know this – **that by deciding to love one another, we love God, and that knowledge came from God.** Pope Francis is getting the same message – but being a humble and holy man – he seems to be applying it to himself and the Catholic Church only; however, Christ came to us and died on the cross for all of our sakes – not His – or only some of us. Christ wanted to show us by his example, unconditional love: **"What so ever you did for one of the least of these brothers and sisters of mine, you did for me"** Matthew 25: 40. God loves all of us with no exceptions or exclusions, and when we decide to exclude any of our brothers or sisters from our love – no matter what we call ourselves – we are excluding God.

One additional thought came to me when I woke up in the middle of the night on December 6, 2014 at 12:01 am – and I feel this thought is so important that I wanted to share it with all my brothers and sisters at the very beginning of my writing; so that if you read nothing else of this message of love from God you will read and give some thought to the following question: **Why would you want to believe that God would teach us a "Golden Rule" – which is for our benefit – and then go on and break his own "Golden Rule"?** The Golden rule is to treat others as you would wish to be treated – isn't it? You then have to believe God would say to us: "Do as I say and not as I do?" And if what a teacher teaches is really important and is truly for the benefit of the student – would any teacher say to the student – "Do as I say and not as I do"? **How could God saying to you "Do as I say and not as I do" make any kind of sense to you?** It is self-evident that where there is love there is peace, and you are with God!

Chapter 1

Love Unifies us with God

Before you read much more of this book, I want to make sure you understand from the beginning that what is contained in this message has come from God through my heart and out of love for all. In no way am I trying to be "holier than thou" or sanctimonious. I am nobody special and still have much to learn. I am just a humble sales person who, as I started to write these thoughts, had been selling paints to contractors and property maintenance painters for forty-three years and was about ready to retire from the paint industry.

In no way is the message I am one of the instruments of delivering to you, trying to reinvent the wheel – the message is just trying to ask you to see for yourself what is going on around you and what works – then put the wheel back on the cart of your life so you may have a smoother ride to your final destination – which is your home with God. Not much of what I am writing in this message is totally new to mankind. My wife had a friend tell her: "Paul and John had it right about what this world needs." And my wife asked: "Who, Paul and John the apostles?" And her friend said: "No, the Beatles Paul and John, when they said all the world needs is love." We have been getting this message of love – and will continue to get this message until many more of us get it. Are we listening yet?

We are to stop leaving the wheels of God's messages of love on the side of the road – which will give our lives a smoother ride. Listen to the good news: God's love does not reject anyone! No matter what others decide to do – try to love your brothers and sisters who are rejecting God. And when they make it hard to do – pray for God's help. Do not believe you are doing God's will when you reject any of your brothers and sisters and exclude them from your love. God's will is for all of us to be an instrument of his love to each other.

Indeed, in no way do I consider myself special or out of the ordinary, yet I do believe that because for the past three years before eating every meal I have been praying the following prayer I am now being called to be God's instrument of his love: **Please Lord, help us to be instruments of your love, for it is in giving that we receive, and in receiving that we give; we are open please bring us to your light and help us to choose the right quantities, and the right types of food, exercise, medicines and sleep for our best health.**

I really do not think of myself as being worthy to truly be an instrument of God's love for all of us, but these thoughts started coming to me when I would wake up in the middle of the night, or sometimes when I was working out. And now to my surprise God is answering my prayer, and of the three things I am being guided to write about – **praying to God is the most powerful of all the messages.** God loves all of us totally unconditionally and mankind thinking otherwise has been getting us into trouble. I have come to realize that when we say God's love is unconditional, it means just that. God's love is without conditions and without exceptions or exclusions. God is love, and because God loves us so much God made us in his image, with the ability of deciding to love; love to be true love has to be chosen, not forced or programed.

This message is a call to action by each one of us as individuals – which can change your own personal world – then go on to be a part of the change which starts the change in the whole world around us by your deciding to love; you can change your world for the better – this is your God-given right. However, you who so choose will find it easier to do if you pray to Our Father in Heaven for help. Some of your brothers and sisters do make it very hard for you to love them.

Robert Palmer released a song in 1986 that became very popular called "Addicted to Love," but an addiction of any sort takes away our free choice, and that kind of love would not be true love. For our love to be a true love it has to be a free choice. However, for a love relationship to become strong there has to be trust in the balance of give and take between the persons involved in the relationship. And trust has to be earned on a moment by moment decision both parties make. If either you or the other person decides to only give or to only receive most of the time, the trust will be broken. The joy and happiness that the relationship brings to both parties will stop growing and eventually go away. To be powerful, giving and receiving should always be two sides of the same coin, love.

I would like to share with you these thoughts that came to me on giving and receiving:

To be powerful, giving and receiving should always be two sides of the same coin, love.

Whether giving or receiving, what will make it powerful is the love intentions of your actions. If you give or receive with humility, love, and appreciation, then God (True Love) will bring you peace, joy, and love. However, if you do either of these things mainly thinking of what you will get out of it for yourself, you will be mostly excluding love for the other person and not bringing yourself closer to God (True Love).

God is love. If you are selfish, what you give or receive will not include what is truly most important and connects you with God, which is love.

You share in God's love when you make the decision to be instruments of God's love without being selfish in giving or in receiving; your decision is then a true love decision. However, true love has to be inclusive of everyone. If you give or receive, and in so doing your action hurts another person, that is not love; when you hurt someone else, you have excluded God (True Love). God has unconditional love for everyone. When you hurt another person, who is also loved by God, your actions have excluded God from your love.

You should note that giving has more power for you than receiving, but only because it always has to be initiated by you, and then the love from God (True Love) comes directly to you. In giving, you demonstrate your appreciation for the gifts and blessings you have already received from God by choosing to share and acknowledge what you have already received from God with others. When you give, God will always send you more love and blessings thanyou can ever possibly give, and so in giving you are also receiving. However, when you allow another person to give to you, you allow the other person to get additional love from God (True Love) by acknowledging and sharing the gifts and blessings they have already received from God with you, and so in receiving you are also giving.

The person giving with humility, love and appreciation receives God's love directly; the person receiving with humility, love and appreciation is receiving God's love indirectly through the person giving.

Giving and receiving are powerful if they are two sides of the same coin, love.

The love intentions of giving and receiving is what Christ is telling us in Mathew 1-16-18; to bring yourself closer to God you have to give and receive without expecting rewards for yourself, but with humility for yourself, and love for the other person: **"Be on guard against performing religious acts for people to see. Otherwise expect no recompense from your heavenly Father."**

In addition, I have come to realize that there are many times when I make it hard for others to love me by my actions, or lack of actions. But by making a conscious decision to demonstrate love, as much as I am able, I make it less difficult for others to cut me a break for my many faults. Like everyone else in the world, I want to be loved. The good news is that God loves us with a greater love than we can ever imagine – totally and unconditionally. You will always have that unimaginable love you can count on no matter how horrible you are with your own decisions. However, if you are horrible with your decisions, you will owe atonement to those you have hurt – to make it easier for them to forgive you. But not to God – forgiveness is always included in God's unconditional love. You do not get to decide which of your brothers and sisters will love you, you only control your own decisions. However, as I said, your own decision can make it easier or harder for others beside God to love you. Even the worst of us sinners want to feel loved by others. But you should know that their decision to love you will always their decision – no matter how much you atone for you misdeeds to them; it will not be your decision to make.

This message would like for you to reflect on why it is so hard for a rich person to be with God. To be with God you have to choose love, and too many times the attitude that has made a person rich, greed and selfishness, will also take you away from choosing love. Giving and receiving are two sides of the same coin, love. It is harder for a rich man to be both wise and humble enough to realize what his **real blessings are** – and to also acknowledge all of **his real blessing came from God**.

Greed and selfishness are the opposites of love because they take you away from the balance of giving and receiving. When you give generously, you should do so with the knowledge that in giving you will also receive; when you choose greed and selfishness you are not choosing love. You should have love, compassion and forgiveness for anyone, including yourself, who chooses the opposite of love. Unless changes are made in those choices, you are moving away from (God) love. Pray for God's help to always choose love so you may enjoy peace and happiness here on earth, and afterwards in your eternal life.

You can make a difference with your actions and change your world for the better or for the worse; our world starts with each one of us; "we are the world" as Michael Jackson and Lionel Richie wrote in their song by that title. Choosing to love changes you for the better and brings you peace, no matter what others decide to do. Love is a decision each of us has to make; you can share love, but not demand it, or steal love when it is not freely given.

Now that I have gotten older I have come to understand that love is the only real treasure we can have in this world. You have to volunteer to give love up. No one can take love away from you. Most of us have heard the expression: "You can't take it with you." It is an expression referring to what happens to possessions and treasures you have accumulated, which you then have to leave behind after you die. Well, the love we hold in our hearts is our only real possession because you will be able to take that treasure with you when you die. In addition, if others remember your love – it will stay behind and never die. Your love will live on through those who remember it, and it might even grow and multiply.

There are three core messages I am trying to share with my readers: **The first is that God loves all of us unconditionally, not just some of us.** God does not exclude anyone from his love, whether we are saints or sinners. We are the ones who do the excluding, and by so doing we are harming our own best interest. You sin against God only because of God's unconditional love for you, or it would not matter to God. God chose to love us first when God created us, but then it is up to each one of us to choose God – or not – by our decision to love God and others. What makes you created in God's image is your ability to make the choice of loving God and others with complete free will.

We need to know that where there is love there is God, and when we choose love we are choosing God – that is the substance of God's message to all of us. That those who say: "God is Great!" are 100 percent right! God will always love us no matter what we do or don't do.

The second is that all of us need to be humble and accept that mankind's spiritual journey has only just begun.

Mac Davis, the American country singer, wrote a song, that many of us who heard it found amusing. It is called, *Oh Lord is Hard to be Humble*. In it he told us that it was hard to be humble because he was perfect in every way. He also told us he was doing the best he could in trying to be humble, and that he never got lonesome "Cause I treasure my own company." He finishes the song with: "To know me is to love me. I must be a hell of a man. Oh Lord is hard to be humble. But I am doing the best I can."

Well, know that the only one who knows you completely is the God who created you – and he does love you. You are perfect in every way in God's love – in everything else – Mac Davis is right in saying you have to do the best you can. And you do have to do the best you can, and never believe for a second you have all the answers. The minute you start to think you have it made – you don't. However, you and I have to keep trying – or we will not reach the full potential God created us to achieve. God wants to help you achieve that potential – but to be truly humble you have to ask for God's help with the knowledge that you will never really know what that full potential might be.

It occurred to me that what Christians celebrate on Christmas is the son of God demonstrating to all of us how love has to be always humble. Who more than our creator is truly perfect in every way? And yet God showed us by His example how love is. Love is always humble.

And if you do not believe Christ was the Son of God – then focus on the substance of what love is. Is love ever arrogant? If you give or receive without being humble – is it love?

Many good people don't find it difficult to be humble as individuals. But very few of us extend the humility we feel as individuals to our own religion's convictions; believing our religion has all the answers, or even most of the answers, is keeping us from growing spiritually.

My spiritual reading, writing, and daily prayers have challenged me to ask questions about many of our beliefs. How are we to know if we are following God's will for us on earth as it is in Heaven? Are we to only read and follow the Holy Books God has given mankind to guide us? And the following is what my prayers to be an instrument of

God's love is telling me. We need to ask these four questions about any of our religions' beliefs – no matter how long those beliefs have been held – and where they have been written: **Does the belief contradict that God's love is for everyone unconditionally? Does this belief call on us to do anything other than a loving act? Does it exclude any of our brothers and sisters? Does it ask us to do anything other than treat others as we would wish to be treated?**

You should know in your heart that if any of your particular beliefs contradict that God loves all of us unconditionally, or cannot be described as calling on us to do a loving act, or does not include all of our brothers and sisters, or does not call on us to treat others as we would wish to be treated, then it could not have come from God; **God is love.** Why would you believe God would have you do anything other than loving acts? Why would you believe God would have you exclude any of your brothers and sisters? Why would you believe God would ever ask you to do anything other than treat others as you would wish to be treated? **"Truly I tell you whatever you did for one of the least of these brothers and sisters of mine, you did for me"** (Matthew 25:40). Yes, even those who do not believe in a higher power but walk the walk of love, and not just talk the talk of love, by deciding to love are bringing God into their lives; **God is the spring where all the love in the universe originated.**

Albert Einstein's definition of insanity is: "doing the same thing over and over again and expecting different results." Ask yourself these questions: how will throwing out any and all of my beliefs that answer any of the four questions I mentioned above with a 'yes' affect my relationship with everyone else and with God? And if I answer no, how does that affect my relationship with everyone else and with God? And if everyone in the whole world throws out their belief that answers 'yes' to any of the four questions, will all of us then be able to get along better because we will then see each other as the brothers and sisters we truly are? Will we then start to have peace on earth? Will we then be doing "God's will on earth as it is in Heaven"? Is it only the other guy's religion that needs to ask those questions, but not mine? Did every bit of my religion originate straight from God and is it completely understood by my religion? Is there nothing more that God needs to send us and teach, which will help us to better understand His will for us? Is there anything new I can possibly learn that will help me to grow spiritually? We are the world, as Michael Jackson and Lionel Richie said in their song; if you decide to change yourself and then take action by throwing out any and all of your beliefs that answers' yes' to the four questions – then you start the process of changing the world. Again, Albert Einstein's definition of insanity is: "doing the same thing over and over again and expecting different results." Don't you see? **People of faith should be the greatest part of the solutions for us to get along with each other, but are we?**

The third, and most important core message, is that prayer works. We need to pray for one another the more we disagree with each other; **it is the message with the most urgency because prayer allows God's unconditional love to connect with us and help us to grow in our spiritual path.** At the end of the day it is always the individual's choice to love or not to love, but God sustains those who pray to see the light of God's love. Prayer works for all of us, not just some of us. In this message, **I want to make clear that what I am writing about does not ask anyone to change their current religion or belief** – or even lack of belief in a higher power – but only to be open to the power of love and to be humble to the fact that mankind's current level of knowledge is but a small fraction of all there is to learn. However, those who lack a belief in a higher power are missing the opportunity to pray for God's help, and God has given all of us complete free will.

All three core messages have one unifying theme, and that unifying theme is love. The closer we come to understanding God's love is for all, the easier it will be to be humble and not exclude any of our brothers and sister who are on their own spiritual path. But our love has to be persistent. We can't give up on any of our brothers and sisters who do not yet understand that love is for their own best interest and that **none of us have but a small fraction of all there is**

for us to learn. Not giving up on love is truly in our own best interest, because it allows God's love to get through to us by the choices we make. In addition, we will find it easier to pray to the one infinite God for help in how to love one another. **God is love, and when we decide to love we are using love as a bridge to connect us to God and to each other.**

John Lennon in his classic song *Imagine* saw the world eventually "coming together as one," and that resonated with many of us no matter our religious beliefs, or even lack of belief. But when John Lennon was asked if he wrote the song as an atheist, the composer said: "no he wrote it as a prayer that Christian denominations would come together" (DND Exclusive publish 12/7/2012).

However, John Lennon missed out by not focusing on one very important element – when he saw the world as being better off without any religion – he left out the tremendous power of prayer when we allow God to help us by choosing to ask for God's help. When you or others are making it hard for you to "come together as one," when you have trouble getting along with others, that is when you can use God's help the most. It is at those times that you need to pray for the best response which will protect you and other innocent people, but that will also take into account God's love for everyone. Yes, even heathen and evil people are loved by God. It is not God rejecting any persons who decides not to love, it is those persons who are rejecting God by their decisions.

It came to me early one morning, as much of what I have been writing comes to me, that I should add a special message of love and celebration for the many people who knew John Lennon personally who are still alive and loved him. I am being guided to let you know that John Lennon is with God. **John Lennon was one of the exceptional rich persons who got it – and he valued the coin of love for others more than any of his other coins. John Lennon was both – a wise and a humble person who realized what was really important in this life – love.**

The power of prayer is the element that some good people, like John Lennon, seem to be missing when they blame religions for keeping us from coming together. **God is love, and deciding to love in our daily lives will bring us closer to God, whether we belong to a particular religion, or no religion.** However, prayer allows God to help us to keep making the decision to love. It is not impossible for an atheist to be loving most of the time, it is just harder because he has to keep choosing to love on his own without being able to ask for God's help when others make it hard to be loving toward them. **But an atheist or an agnostic, who sees everyone – with no exceptions – as his brother and sister gets the substance of God's message of love; it does not matter whether he realizes it or not. "Ask and it shall be given you"** (Matthew 7:7) is the important part that he is missing. All of us have the God-given right to choose love. And those good people who blame religion for not allowing us to come together would "throw out the baby with the bath water," as an old idiomatic expression states. It does not matter to God, because he loves all of us unconditionally, how we pray for his help. God will listen to the Native American praying to the "Great Spirit" for guidance; or to the devout Muslim who prays in the direction of Mecca, or any of our brothers and sisters who open their hearts as best they can in trying to connect with God. It is not religions that are keeping us apart, or the people with those religions. It is those people not being humble about their belief. It is those who do not accept that they don't have all the answers to the greatness of an infinite God, and also those who respond to the four simple questions in a positive way to some of their core belief: **Does the belief contradict that God's love is for everyone unconditionally? Does this belief call on us to do anything other than a loving act? Does it exclude any of our brothers and sisters? Does it ask us to do anything other than treat others as we would wish to be treated?**

Do not let any of your beliefs imagine God has anything but unconditional and unimaginable love for all of us. Many of the spiritual books I have been reading tell us that we can't pick and choose what we want to believe from the Holy books we have been handed down, but we need to stop believing the part of anyone's beliefs that conflict with God being the source of all love in our universe.

God created us with free will, so yes, each one of us has the God-given right to pick and choose what we want to believe from any of our Holy books – **and if it means you not choosing love over anything written in a Holy book – you have to! You have to choose love if you want to choose God. God is love. And it is your God-given right to choose love!** Believing anything that contradicts God's love for us as unconditional, or that somehow God would want us to do anything but loving acts, to do anything but include all of our brothers and sisters, or do anything other than to treat others as we wish to be treated is what is taking us away from God's will for us "on earth as it is in heaven." **When you choose to love you are choosing God because God is the spring where all the love in our universe originated.**

So again, in no way is this message asking anyone to throw out **all of their beliefs**; I am not throwing out all of mine. My son Marc told me about a metaphor which he was told when taking a ten day meditation retreat: **"If you are hungry and you find a small stone in your bowl of cereal, you do not take the whole bowl of cereal and dump it on the ground, you go ahead and pick the stone out of your bowl, and then eat the cereal in your bowl."** This message would just like you to reflect on the four basic questions about those beliefs mentioned above – we should know in our hearts that God loves us unconditionally, and that if any of our particular beliefs contradicts that God love is unconditional, or cannot be described as a loving act, or does not include all of our brothers and sisters, or does not treat others as we would wish to be treated – then the beliefs could not have come from God – because God is love. And in addition, reflect on where God wants all of mankind to go in their spiritual journey – which now that we know how long the Universe has been around – it has truly just begun. I am getting this very strong message from God that I want to share with you: **What part of loving all your brothers**

and sisters is it that we do not understand? This message also had unimaginable love in it.

As I am setting out to send this message of love to as many people as possible – in which the most important core message is the power of prayer – a friend sent me, in an e-mail, the following thoughts by Phillips Brooks, an Episcopal clergyman and author who lived in the Nineteenth century:

Do not pray for easy lives. Pray to be stronger people.

Do not pray for tasks equal to your powers.

Pray for powers equal to your tasks.

I also want to share the following thought that was written when I was around ten years old about hell. But please believe it has always been your decision to make – and not God's which will send you there:

> "It takes two to love. It takes liberty. It takes the right to reject. If there were no hell, we would be like the animals. No hell, no dignity."
>
> – Flannery O'Connor, 1959

Chapter 2

My father and I chased after a bicycle-riding bully. Do we need to have a hearing test?

In 1959 when I was ten years old there was this kid who at the time was twelve; this twelve-year-old kid started picking on me and pushing me around. There is a big difference in the physical development of a ten-year-old and a twelve-year-old boy. The twelve-year-old boy was on his way to becoming a man, but I was still just a kid. I remember running home crying, and on finding my father, I told him that I was being picked on by a bigger kid than me. My father asked me: "Where is this kid?" So I told him he was probably still in our neighborhood, and maybe we could find him. We jumped into my father's car and started driving around the neighborhood where we lived, and then I saw him, riding his bicycle almost a block away. "There he is!" I yelled at my father. So my father accelerated the car and turned the corner chasing right after that kid and his bike. However, just as we went around the corner we saw that the kid, figuring he was not going to be able to outrun our car, darted into an alley. By the time we drove around to the other side of the block, that kid was nowhere to be found. I told my father I was really sorry he got away, and then I asked him: "What were you going to do to him?" thinking my father was going to beat up the bully for picking on me, or at least give him a lecture and maybe take him home to his parents so they could teach him not to pick on someone smaller than he was. But my father told me: *I was going to let the two of you work out your differences, without any interference from anybody.* I remember thinking: *Boy, I am sure glad we didn't catch him! What was my father thinking? I thought he was on my side, not the bully.*

It is with love and humility that I would like to suggest that it is the attitude that "God is on my side, not the other guy's," that has gotten us into so much trouble, and it should be self- evident by now that God's message is that he loves all of us, whether we are sinners or saints. It is for each one of us to decide to love God or reject God; it is by your decision to love that you receive more love in return from God. Or by your choice not to love that you are rejecting the love God wants to give to you. I believe you should try reaching out to God by praying together for each other's good will toward one another, because it will demonstrate your wish to follow God's will for love and peace, and you are asking for God's help. Those of us who are trying to grow closer to God have witnessed the power of prayers. However, it is up to each one of us to realize that to love others is in your own best interest. We can ask for God's help by praying to God for his light to show us a better way to love each other; it will not matter how you pray or in what language. If your intention for praying has love for the other person as its main ingredient, God will answer your prayers; God's love is for all. That you are to choose love has been the "good news" God has been trying to get you to understand for a very long time in the past, now, and forevermore. Please keep in mind, however, that at the end of the day it has always been your decision, not God's. The bottom line you need to get to is realizing it is for your own best interest, not the other guy's that you are called to love. Realizing it is your best interest to love others. It will allow you to love them anyway, regardless of what the other person's decision ends up being. We can hate the sin, but love and have compassion for the sinner; it will not matter if that sinner ends up being you, or the other person.

You always want the other guy to do the right things, but find excuses for when you are the one who does wrong. You forget that peace on earth has to begin with each individual taking full responsibility for their actions and doing the right things, especially when it is hard. He who said the other guy is always completely wrong is going to be wrong most of the time he acts in that spirit. He will not only be wrong, but will also miss out on a chance to find common ground with the other person. In addition, he might miss out on a chance to get a better understanding of his own core principles and beliefs.

The above incident with the bicycle riding bully happened when I was around ten years old in 1959, and it was also 1959 when this thought was written about hell:

"It takes two to love. It takes liberty. It takes the right to reject. If there were no hell, we would be like the animals. No hell, no dignity."
– Flannery O'Connor, 1959

I like to humbly share with you these thoughts touched on by Pope Francis at his Installation Mass of March 19, 2013 on St. Joseph's Feast. **Every person matters!** And when anyone speaks with tenderness and affection to others – the person speaking, irrespective of his or her religious affiliation or doctrine – is acting as an instrument of God's love to all. That "every person matters" is the same very strong message that I want to share with you: **Why is it we do not want to believe God's love is for all of us, with no exceptions?** Pope Francis' theme touched upon how each and every person is important:

> It means protecting people, showing concern for each and every person, especially children, the elderly, those in need, the one who are often the last we think about. It means caring for one another in our families: husband and wives first protect one another, and then as parents, they for their children, and children themselves, in time, protect their parents. It means building sincere friendships in which we protect one another in trust, respect, and goodness. In the end, everything has been entrusted to our protection, and all of us are responsible for it. Be protectors of God's gifts!

I am writing these thoughts out of love, and with humility, knowing that only to the extent that I stay true to my intentions of love and humility will there be any truth in my words that will resonate and be a spark in uniting us to be instruments of God's love.

I am mentioning several "coincidences" that happened while writing this message, not because writing this message makes me special, my message is that we are all special in the eyes of God. The "coincidences" are to demonstrate the message is special and you should believe the importance of the message that we are all loved equally and unconditionally by God, and that we are all special to God

It is hard for anyone to understand, but I would like to ask you to consider what is involved in unconditional love: **With unconditional love justice is a given, you can't have unconditional love for someone and not be just to them. Mercy is a given, you can't have unconditional love for someone and not give them mercy. Forgiveness is a given, you can't have unconditional love for someone and not give them forgiveness – they are all contained in that kind of love – or it would have conditions!**

Do we need to have a hearing test?

When a friend, who is a hearing aid specialist, gave me a hearing test he said the word "hunt," and I thought I repeated back "hunt," but he heard "hut," so he thought I was the one not hearing correctly. This is what I believe has happened with the message God has been trying to give us. He has been trying to tell us one thing, but we hear another. One of the very strong messages I am getting is that all of us need to focus on God's messages of love, not on the messengers; so when in John 14: 6 "I am the way and the truth, and the life no one comes to the Father but through me. If you really knew me, you would know my Father also. From this point on you know him; you have seen him." God was speaking of his message of love that he sent his son to us to deliver, not the messenger. God did not send his son to be one of us for God's benefit, but for our sake; God wanted to show us how to make the choice to be with him, on earth as it is in heaven. Why would Christ tell us to turn the other cheek if someone strikes us, and then do anything other than love all of us unconditionally? Sending someone to hell does not sound very loving does it?

In John 3: 16 **"That whoever believes in him may not die but may have eternal life"** we were supposed to hear God's message, but most of us heard Christ – not God's message of love. The same thing with John 10: 9 **"I am the gate. Whoever enters through me will be safe. He will go in and out and find pasture."** And again I believe God was telling us to focus on his message when in John 10: 16 we were told **"I have other sheep that do not belong to this fold. I must lead them too, and they shall hear my voice. There shall be one flock then, one shepherd."**

I have noticed much more love coming into my life since I started writing and sharing my thoughts. The process of trying to put into practice the words I have written; to not "just talk the talk," but to also do the walk is helping me connect with God's love. How delighted I would be if more of my brothers and sisters would also start to pray to be instruments of God's love; our world needs all the love we can get. My prayer to be an instrument of God's love has made me become more aware of God's love for each and every one of us, with no exceptions or exclusions. I know more about myself not being worthy than about anyone else, but that is the message God has been trying to get us to understand. **God's love for all of us is totally unconditional.** However, it is always our choice to accept God's love or not.

I have also noticed that my prayers have helped me to feel much more connected with God. It is as if God is standing behind my shoulders as I take a test in school and is just waiting for me to ask, to then be able to provide me with all the answers on how to deal with any and all of my life's problems.

In praying to be an instrument of God's love we are in effect praying for God to help us be open to God's love; "for it is in giving that we receive, and receiving that we give." If all you do is receive love, you are allowing others to be open to God's love, but keeping yourself from receiving God's love directly. You can receive love without choosing to receive love and allow others to be instruments of God's love. But to give love and thereby be open to receive God's love directly, you will always have to be the one making the decision to give love.

Those who give love to others are becoming instruments of God's love to others and they are receiving God's love directly for themselves. But those who choose not to give love are choosing to move away from God.

Our science now tells us that people with low self-esteem find it hard to give love. Is it because you need to love yourself first to be able to **"love your neighbor as yourself"**? (Mark 12:31) **God is love, and when we decide to love we are using love as a bridge to connect us to God and to each other.**

Our ability to give love or to choose not to give love was given to us by God when He created us. God is the fountain of all love, and God chose to love us.

All of us are called to make judgments about love moment by moment; we need to be aware that the harder the decision is to make, the more we should reach out for God's help with our prayers. If we make the wrong decision, we can sometimes totally destroy what has taken us a life time to build. We do not want to make the wrong decision when the love for our brothers and sisters is involved in our decision, especially for the helpless ones. Joe Paterno, the famous Penn State University football coach, once said: "Success without honor is an unseasoned dish, it will satisfy your hunger, but it will not taste good." However we now know that when Joe Paterno was called to make the most important decision he would ever have to make, to defend helpless children who were being abused, Joe made the wrong decision. Joe Paterno did not defend the helpless children that were being abused. Joe therefore tarnished his brilliant lifetime legacy of both success and honor.

There have been some who have otherwise answered God's call to love, but who have also made the wrong decision when the love for some of our brothers and sisters should have been the deciding factor, especially for the helpless. Like Joe Paterno, they were called to make the most important decision they would ever have to make, to defend helpless children that were being abused, and they too made the wrong decision. Therefore they also tarnished what might have been brilliant legacies of both success and honor. We can hate the sin, but love and have compassion for the sinner, whether that sinner ends up being you or the other person. You always want the other guy to do the right things, but find it easy to make excuses for when you do wrong. We forget that God's call to love has to begin with each individual taking full responsibility for their actions and doing the right things, especially when it is hard.

Again, it is with love and humility that I hope you can see for yourself that deciding to love is in your best interest and not for those who you decide to love. If you decide to love you can make an immediate change for the better in your own personal life and also start the process of changing for the better your own part of the world. I would humbly also like for all of us to look around at our world and at what mankind has done thus far, and ask ourselves this question: Is this the best that we can do?

I would like to conclude chapter two of my book with this thought expressed by the Chinese philosopher Laozi (c 604 BC – c531): "The longest journeys start with the first step." So the first step is to realize that God is love, and when you decide to love you are using love as a bridge to connect you to God and others.

God has unconditional love for each and every one of us, and when we choose to love others because we realize we are all brothers and sisters under our creator, we are able to open the bridge that allows us to receive the great love and joy God wants us to have. You are choosing to join with God in the love he has for all of us and thereby you receive the great love and joy God wants you to choose for yourselves. It is why Christ called on all of us to love our enemies, and to love others as we love ourselves. Unconditional love is the choice God wants you to make, but will not force you to make. Forced love would not be true love.

Chapter 3

Mankind's spiritual journey has only just begun; a child and his bowl at the edge of an infinity ocean.

Throughout history mankind has learned that what we believe does not actually change the nature of the universe or God, but only ourselves. The earth did not change from being flat to round when mankind discovered it was really round. It was round all along. And mankind should have also learned by now that the earth is not the center of the universe – and has never been.

In my humble opinion mankind should be able to act with complete humility with the knowledge we now have, and know without any doubt or questions how little we do know about the nature of the universe – let alone about the creator of that universe. We are not the center of the universe. But yet many of us do not act that way, and not acting that way is keeping us from achieving our full potential.

I remember my brother Manuel, who is a year older than me, telling me when he was six or seven years old, that looking at how messed up the world was, children should rule the world. Children would be open to new answers to all the problems of the world; the adults in charge did not seem to want to change, and they were making a big mess of things by refusing to change – or we would not be having wars all the time. We were children who in our ignorance believed we had all the answers, but in reality we did have one important part of the answer – something has to change. My brother is a grandfather and much wiser now, but he knows that even as children we could see that doing the same things and expecting different results was never going to improve things. Manuel has earned two master's degrees, and he now knows how little he really knows. My brother has become a very wise person because he knows that **a wise person stops being wise the minute he believes he has all the answers, and there is not much more for him to learn.**

For anyone of us, or any group of us, to believe we know all there is to know about the nature of the universe, or the nature of God, would be like a child who goes to the ocean shore and pours some of the ocean water into a wooden bowl and then says to himself, "The ocean is in my bowl." There is truth in that statement, but not all of the truth. Some of the ocean is in the bowl, but not even close to the entire ocean is in the child's bowl. And then another child comes to the same ocean shore and fills his bowl with the ocean water, and then starts fighting with the first child because he believes only his bowl has the ocean in it, and how dare the first child say it is his bowl that has the ocean in it. How silly is that?

If the children of this world want to know which of their bowls contain more of God in them they should look at what is in those bowls and see which of those bowls have the most love in them; when all of our bowls have nothing but love in them, "the world will be together as one" (Michael Jackson and Lionel Richie, We are the World song), and **"God's will be done on earth as it is in heaven"** (Mathew 6:10).

I like to share with you one of my most important inspirations that came to me while writing my thoughts, and is very relevant as to why in the past I would find myself at a dead end: Success is a journey not a destination. If I refuse to give up – I am already successful. However, success is also realizing I can always do better; that I need to pray to find a way to be a better me not only when things are going wrong, but when they are going right! The minute I start to believe I am as good as I will ever be and I have it made – I won't!

The truth of an infinite God, who created an infinite universe, cannot possibly be contained in any one religion. Look for the love and there you will find God, but also know that all the religions of the world put together, never mind just one, can only have but a small portion of an infinite God.

It is with love and humility that I would like to suggest we should be wiser by now than we were two thousand years ago. Mankind then, was just like that child filling his bowl by the ocean; mankind was starting to understand the universe we live in. But it was the belief of thinking we knew more than we actually knew, that held us back for several centuries from learning more about the true nature of the universe. Compare to how long we now know the universe has been around, we just got here two seconds ago. Spiritually, as a child would ask the question: "Are we there yet?" Our answer should be: "No, we are just starting, but at least no longer completely lost."

It was only during the Renaissance period, when mankind started to become more open to how much there was yet for us to learn, that progress was made. Our scientific knowledge is now growing by leaps and bounds because we know how small our knowledge of the universe is in comparison to what we now know there is still for us to learn. So why do we seem unable to admit that we know as much, or as little, about the creator of our universe? Why do we imagine we know more about the creator of the universe than we know about the universe? By now mankind should know enough to know the true miracles of all of God's creations. On the other hand, why do some of us seem to look for more miracles to demonstrate God existence? We should know enough by now to see those miracles all around us. I would humbly like for all of us to look around at our world and at what mankind has done thus far, and ask ourselves this question: Is this the best that we can do? We are like the child that fills his bowl with the ocean water and tells himself he holds the entire ocean in his bowl.

Mankind should be able to see that the very existence of God does not have to be taken on faith by any one of us anymore. We know the universe has been around for billions of years, but mankind has only been around for the very smallest of fraction of that time. We now know how complicated the universe is, and we know how complicated living things are. And in addition, we also know how all these things work in perfect harmony. It is not logical to imagine the universe and life work the way we know they work by pure coincidence. It is also not logical to imagine mankind, let alone just some of us, know all we need to know about the creator of that very complex and infinite universe.

It is with love and humility that I would like to suggest that we now also know that some of these very basic principles God has been trying to teach us are practical principles that will work for you, right here and right now, for those who choose to follow them. That it is in giving that you receive and in receiving that you give. It is always your choice when you give, but sometimes people will give to you without you asking them to do so. When you allow others to give to you, you are also giving to them. However, in receiving God's blessing of love through others who decide to give to you, you are accepting an obligation to initiate your own giving. Because you have received God's love indirectly through another person, you have to then pass on God's love to others even more then when you were the one who initiated the giving. You are taking on an obligation to demonstrate to God you do not take those loving gifts you are receiving for granted. And that you will find a way to pass the love you have received on to others. **But you still have an obligation to pass on God's love, when it is God who is directly blessing you or your family without you asking for his blessings.** In addition, to love our enemies means that you need to keep your heart open to the fact that we are all brothers and sisters in the eyes of our creator. That what makes you, **"created in God's image"** (Genesis 1:27), is your ability to choose to love your brothers and sisters as God loves each and everyone one of us. **"His will be done on earth as it is in heaven"** (Matthew 6:10), means keeping your hearts open and choosing to love everyone whether they choose to love you or not. All who decide not to love are moving themselves away from God's love, and it is always your own choice to make and no one else's. My brother Manuel told me the other day: "we can love an inanimate object like a robot or a car, but they are not able to choose to love us back, only be programed to do so." It is our ability to choose to love that makes us **"created in God's image"** (Genesis 1:27). God chose to love us first, in John 4:19 **"We love because he first loved us."** God is love, and when we decide to love we are using love as a bridge to connect us to God and to each other.

So let me please ask for the love and the understanding of my brothers and sisters from other religions and traditions when I speak from my heart about God's love message to all of us. I will speak mostly from my own imperfect knowledge of the Christian tradition. The good news, as we who hold that particular bowl from the ocean say, is that God loves all of us and this has always been the truth; the truth that God is love, and hell is not is just as true as the truth that the earth has always been round and not flat. Let us look into our own knowledge of our own religion, or no religion, and know that where there is love there is God. Please do not just listen to words, but open your heart to love and see how powerful love is, and that love has to come from our creator.

History tells us that mankind's holy books were actually written over periods of hundreds of years, and yet we now seem to think that spiritually we have all that we need to learn in those books already, and it is holding us back from growing; I have always said: **the minute a person thinks they have it made, they don't.** Believing you have all the answers will keep you from learning all that there is yet to be learned. It does not mean you throw out all that are in those holy books, but being humble to the fact that mankind's journey in the universe has only just begun. There is much that yet needs to be written for us to truly understand the basic principles contained in those holy books. Please look around at our world and at what mankind has done up until now, and ask yourselves this question: Are we anywhere close to doing God's will on earth as it is in heaven?

I would like to suggest to all of my brothers and sisters that although there are many who are humble as individuals, almost none are humble about their particular bowl from the ocean not holding the entire ocean that is God. Not being humble about this fact has been getting mankind into trouble. Mankind's spiritual journey has only just begun, and the more of us who come to acknowledge this, the easier it will be to love all of our brothers and sisters. We are all on the same spiritual journey; acknowledging we are all just starting the journey will make it easier to pray for each other with love and humility.

Mankind will probably never be able to fill any of our bowls with the entire ocean. However, giving up trying because the task is never going to be finished would be just as bad as believing – as we seem to do – that there is no need to try filling our bowl with more of the ocean. If you pray – your bowls will be filled with as much as you need from God.

I would like to suggest that the paradigm of your universe needs to change, because it is keeping you from achieving your full potential. If you believe you have already arrived at your spiritual destination, you will stop a journey that in truth has only just begun. We are making progress in our journey, but knowing now just how long mankind has been around in comparison to how long the universe has been around should keep us from believing we have already arrived. But somehow it does not seem to do so, and it is holding us back. Do you really believe that this is the best that mankind will ever achieve spiritually? I hope not, because we basically just got here, in comparison to how long the universe has been around.

I would also like to suggest to you that we are now past the stage where humanity needs to take anything or everything on just total faith. We now know enough to truly know how much we don't know. None of us need to throw out all of our water from our bowl and say that was not the ocean; rather than doing that what we need to admit is that it never was the entire ocean we were holding in our bowl. Whatever religion you believe in, whether that religion is Jewish, Christian, Buddhist, Hindu, the Great Spirit, or Mother Nature you will not be able to achieve your full potential until you admit to yourselves that your particular bowl, or any of your brothers and sisters' bowls, does not hold the entire waters of the infinite ocean that is God.

This is not a new message, a friend told me about a movie made several years ago, with George Burns playing God called "Oh God," and in the movie God was on trial; God was asked if Jesus was his son, and God said yes, but so were Buddha, and Mohammad and many others in human history. The message of the movie was the same as the message I am getting, that God does not belong to just one church; God belongs to any and all of the churches where there is love because God loves all of us. God is bigger than any of our bowls, or our entire bowls put together, never mind just one, if we think otherwise we are just like the child at the shore of the ocean who thinks he holds the entire ocean in his bowl. **It is the substance of the messages – not the messengers which is important for all of us to believe.**

One of the books I read while writing this paper is *Joy to the World. How Christ's Coming Changed Everything (And Still Does)* by Scott Hann. In this book Scott Hann makes the case for the importance of Christ coming to our world. I believe that Mr. Hann and many Christians are correct regarding the importance of Christ coming to our world. However, the message I am being called to share with all of you is that the importance of Christ coming to the world we should focus on is that God's message of love for all of us is so important that he sent his Son to demonstrate the importance of the message. God sent his Son to us to show us by his example how we are to love each other if we are to love God. Scott Hann quotes in his book: (Mathew 12:48-50) **"Who is my mother? Who are my brothers?" Then extending his hand towards his disciples, he said "There are my mother and my brothers. Whoever does the will of my heavenly Father is brother and sister and mother to me."** Scott Hann also said in this book that **"God drew close so that we could see clearly – and know that 'God is love'** (1 John 4:8, 16). In eternity, that is his deepest identity. Before he created anything to love, he was love; and love is an act that requires both a subject and object, a lover and a beloved. God is that pure act of love." Mr. Hann then also quotes Pope Francis letter titled *The Joy of the Gospel.*

> The joy of the Gospel is for all people: no one can be excluded. That is what the angel proclaimed to the shepherds in Bethlehem: **"Be not afraid; for behold, I bring you good news of a great joy which will come to all the people"** (Luke 2: 10).

The Christian religion I have grown up with will call each other "my brothers and sisters in Christ," when what we should all say is "my brothers and sister in God." The simple truth that you should know in your heart is that God created an infinite universe, and that all of us in that universe who have the ability to choose to love are God's children; therefore you should want to include all of God's children who live in that infinite universe. **However, I need to make clear to you, that if any of your brothers and sisters call God by some other name – or even if they do not believe or acknowledge God – they are still your brothers and sisters because there is only one God who created all of us, and who loves us unconditionally. Most parents' love for their children is totally unconditional – and what the child call his, or her, parent – matters only to the child.** Why would you want to exclude those of God's children – who are also your brothers and sisters – just because they do not acknowledge Christ as being one and the same with God? **Did Christ ask you to exclude any of your brothers and sisters from your love?**

Our current stage of development should allow us to see and to know in very practical down to earth terms that what God has been asking us to take on faith at an earlier stage of mankind's development works when we follow those principles; science is now catching up to those principles, but they were true principles all along.

Many religions, including the Christian religion, call on mankind to love each other and to love God. These religions also have the concept that God with his unconditional love for all of us will someday judge us and decide to send us to hell if we have not followed his commandments. These religions believe that those who do not believe in the water from their own particular bowl also have a much greater chance to be sent to hell by God. Believing it is somehow God, and not ourselves who are the one making the choice to move away from God's love is keeping us from better understanding and loving all of our brothers and sisters in the world. God is love, and when we decide to love we are using love as a bridge to connect us to God and to each other.

I was ready to go ahead and send out what I had already written; because I was starting to feel a sense of urgency in sending out this message. I know my message is far from perfect. However, my hope in sending it out is to just really send out a spark of God's love in the hope that others will expand on my thoughts and add to my own spiritual journey that has only just begun.

However, I am now adding this paragraph that I had not written until just now. Today I have just come back from church, and the message I heard on the reading of the Gospel on July 7, 2013 (Luke 10), fits so well with the message I am receiving about God being love, but hell is not. **In the Gospel God was asking his disciples to go into people's homes and tell them peace be with you, and that if the people who owned the homes accepted the peace, peace would be on to them, but if they did not accept the peace wish, the peace would just come back to those who had asked for the peace.** I became overwhelmed with joy and love in church because I know that I am not worthy to hear God's message of peace and love, let alone try to send it out to others. But I do so anyway because I know that regardless of any of us being worthy, God does wish peace and love unto all of us. God with his unconditional love does think all of us are worthy. We are all his children no matter what choices we make, or even if we do not believe God exists. However, by not believing in God we are missing the opportunity of asking for God's help when life's problems arise and we need extra help. It is those who do not accept God's message of peace and love who are the ones missing out on true happiness, and those who give out the message of peace and love will get that peace and love returned to them regardless of which particular bowl they draw their ocean water from.

It is with love and humility that I would like all of us to think about the contradiction in the message that God would send us to hell if we do not believe in his love. Does that make sense? Is it logical? The God that asked us to love our enemies, the God that said: **"let he who is without sin throw the first stone"**(John 8:7), that the same God who asked us to forgive those who trespass against us as we would want to be forgiven, would then also send us to eternal punishment when we have trespassed against his commandments?

Mankind should be able to see the power of love in action. Why would we imagine that our creator has anything other than love for us? When Christ died on the cross, and he asked for forgiveness for those who were crucifying him; he was asking us by his example, to forgive those who choose not to love us because they do not yet understand that love gives more to those who give it, than to those who receive it. Why else would Christ have asked for forgiveness for those who were crucifying him? Does it make sense Christ would have asked for forgiveness for those who did not understand what they were doing, and then at a later date send them all to hell?

God is love, and Hell is not; a message of Love to all. God wants us to love because it is self-evident that loves brings happiness to those who give love. God wants us to love because God loves us. It is also self-evident that choosing not to love never makes those who so choose happy. Has anyone ever met a totally selfish person who radiated happiness? However, most of us have met loving, giving persons who radiated happiness. And we ourselves, when we give love feel our own hearts filling with joy. We do not have to take these things on faith anymore; we can see these things for ourselves, right here, and right now that these things are true.

I would like to suggest to you, that it makes more sense, and creates no contradictions to see hell as what we create when we decide not to love. It is those who choose not to love that send themselves there, not God. You do not have to take anyone's word for this; you can see it when people are currently sent to prison that what makes prison such a terrible place is that there are some people there who only care about what is good for them. These people care only for themselves and never anyone else. Society is concentrating these kinds of people in one place, and that is one of the things we need to change because it reinforces the belief those people have that the way to get along in this world is to do harm unto others before they do it to you. We have made progress from the way we used to treat our prisoners, but we can, and should do better. Demonstrating love for others does more for those who are demonstrating the love, than for those who are the recipient of the love. But those receiving God's blessing of love are also accepting an even larger obligation to pass on God's love than those who are the ones initiating the giving. However, deciding to give love or receive love is always your choice to make, and in your own best interest.

I would like to share a message with you that I received the other day that reinforced my thoughts regarding the fact that it is our decision to be close to God or move away from the light of his love, not God's. This message totally resonated with me; I hope it also does with you. I was with one of my friends the other day, and I told him about the message I had gotten that day: **God does not choose saints, saints choose God**. Well, it also came to me the next morning that I needed to share **the good news that the converse is also true: that God does not reject sinners, sinners reject God**. When sinners decide not to love, they are rejecting God's love. God does not choose any of his saints in particular, but is asking for all of us to be saints by choosing love. God wants every single one of us to be saints and not sinners – not for others' sake – but your own. However, do not confuse vocations with being saints, vocations are truly God's calling according to the God-given talent you have received; there can be saints who are healers, or builders, scientists, and yes even salespersons. Some of us have failed to understand **"You did not choose me, but I**

chose you" (John 15:16). What I believe this means is that God chose to love us when he first created us, but then it is up to you to decide to love God and others and thereby become saints; it is truly in your best interest to do this because it will bring you joy and peace by bringing you closer to God. Again, do not confuse vocations with being saints, **no one can prevent you from choosing to be a saint,** but as we have seen throughout history – and even to this day – some will prevent others from following the vocation God is calling on them to follow by the God-given talent they have received. To be any kind of saint, however, one has to be consistent in a moment by moment decision to love. All saints I have ever heard of use God to help them stay the course of their decision to love by praying for his help. **Saints do not pray a lot because they are saints; they are saints because they pray a lot.** Therefore, continue to decide to love, and pray for God's help to stay consistent with the decision – because when you so choose – you will be with God.

His will be done, on earth as it is in heaven, is for us to decide to love. God loves every one of us, saints or sinners. God is truly love, and it is those who choose not to love, that send themselves to hell, right here and right now, and then later in their eternal life of their souls. God is love, and when we decide to love we are using love as a bridge to connect us to God and to each other.

That God is love for every one is the "good news" mankind does not understand and it is getting us into trouble. Believing that God's love is only for those who share our own particular bowl is getting us into trouble. It should have been clear, after more than two thousand years that what God has been calling all of us, not just some of us, to do is to love all of our brothers and sisters, whether we consider them saints or sinners; it is in each one of our own best interests that God is calling us to love. God did not reject historical sinners like Hitler, Hitler rejected God. God would have welcomed even Hitler to the light of his love had Hitler made the decision to stop his evil ways and reached out to the light of God's love; this is truly "good news" for the rest of us who might feel too unworthy of God's love because of our own past misdeeds. God's love for all of us is so unconditional that it was Hitler who rejected God's love, not God who rejected Hitler. The evil that Hitler did on this earth was Hitler's choice, not God's. It then follows that when you decide to love, you are doing God's will, on earth as you will also do in heaven.

It should also have been self-evident by now that it is those who decide not to love who are sending themselves away from God's light of love and into the darkness of hell. God is love, and hell is not; is God's message of love to all.

One of the basic principles God is hoping we learn is that if you do not forgive those who have trespassed against you, you harm yourself far more than you harm those you do not forgive. In many cases those who harmed you are not even alive, but yet you keep love from coming into your life by holding on to your bitterness toward those who did you wrong. It is with love and humility I like to suggest you leave the past in the past; you can only change what is in the "now" or present moment. You can't change what was, you can only change what will be, and that goes double for when the one you need to forgive, is yourself. I have read this basic principle in both the Bible and in the Qur'an, but I am sure it is also in many of mankind's holy books because it is such a basic principle that God has been trying to get us to learn.

Chapter 4

LOVE IS A MOMENT BY MOMENT CHOICE – WHICH IS ALWAYS IN OUR BEST INTEREST

I would like to share with you a personal experience I had a few years ago as to how judging a relationship we had with someone in our past by how we remember the relationship, rather than reaching out to the person, can keep love out of our lives: My aunt "Nena" was celebrating her ninetieth birthday and our family in Miami Florida, where she lived, wanted to give her a big surprise party. They contacted all her relatives throughout the United States, not just the locals, and asked if we wanted to be there to surprise her and help her celebrate her ninetieth birthday. When I received the invitation I told my brother Manuel, that I did not know if I wanted to go through all the hassle of driving all the way from where I live in Annapolis, Maryland to where my brother lived at the time in Fredericksburg,Virginia, and then drive together all the way to Miami.

When my brother Manuel and I were growing up, I remember my aunt Nena being very stern with both of us, and telling us that if we did not change our ways, we were going to end up in jail. My brother and I were probably less than ten years old when my aunt told us this. At the time of my aunt's ninetieth birthday we were both in our fifties, and yet after all those years that was what I remembered about my aunt. Well my brother and my wife Patty were instruments of God's love and talked me into going anyway, that it was the right thing to do.

The following is what I remember about my aunt's ninetieth birthday: My aunt Nena being brought into a large party room, and everyone yelling surprise, but what truly made me feel not worthy of my aunt's love, was how one of the first things she did in that crowded room full of people was to come to me and said: "Alejandrito, I am so happy to see you," as tears were coming to her eyes, "this is such a happy thing that you are here to be with me," and then she hugged me. I felt like the prodigal son must have felt when he was welcomed back home by his father, not worthy of such unconditional love (Luke 15:11-32). My aunt passed away four years later and left each of her nieces and nephews a few thousand dollars inheritance, including me. To this day I am very happy, that I decided to be there with my aunt to celebrate her ninetieth birthday. I am ashamed that I almost missed out on a very joyous day, not only for my aunt Nena, but also for me; I almost missed out witnessing my aunt Nena's love for me. I realize now that in receiving God's blessing of love through my aunt Nena who decide to give her love to me, I was also accepting an even larger obligation to pass on God's love to others.

We need to be open to love because we never know when love will knock on our door, and if we do not open the door we will be the losers. Before I met my wife Patty, I used to pray: "Please lord, bring a woman into my life that will help me be the best me that I can be," and without a doubt, when I look at how much both of us have grown spiritually, my wife Patty and I have helped each other become better persons. My wife Patty is an amazing person, and I have no doubt that it was God that brought her into my life. We met because my younger sister was going to a Catholic High School with Patty, and my sister invited Patty to go on a family trip to New York. My father had just received the gift of a brand new VW bus from my oldest sister and our family was going to test it out by going on a family trip to New York. On the way to New York the brand new VW bus engine started overheating, and a tow truck had to be called to tow us back to the nearest town. My father decided we were not going to be able to continue our family trip and got us tickets to go back home in a Greyhound bus. Patty was sitting across the aisle from me, and next to my sister. We started to talk, and there was this very intense attraction between us. My sister told Patty, after seeing how much we were enjoying talking with each other, that she wanted to get some sleep, and why didn't Patty go ahead and move over and sit next to me? I was at the time almost ready to break up with a current girlfriend. And as soon as we got back from our trip, I broke up with her, and then started dating Patty. I know that we met because of my prayers, and that we were meant to help each other become better persons. However, we have only just begun our spiritual journey, and we also have to decide, on a moment by moment ongoing basis, to continue choosing to love each other. At the time we met, Patty was going to go to school to become a Registered Nurse, and after the second year of going to nursing school, we got married. I was able to be there to help her complete her studies to become a Registered Nurse. There is no doubt in my mind, after over forty-seven years since the incident I described of how we met, and forty-four years of marriage to Patty – we have both grown spiritually because of helping each other throughout our lives together. God truly answered my prayers when He brought Patty into my life. Our journey has only just begun.

I have learned to be more loving and compassionate from my wife Patty. Patty worked in the intensive care unit of really sick new babies, when she first started working as a nurse, and then in the office of a Pediatrician, and then later in her career also worked with patients at the end of life, with home hospice. Patty is currently working with a company whose mission is to call people with chronic diseases, and try to help them stay on track with the things they are supposed to be doing to better manage their disease. God has used Patty's career path in nursing like a school of life's lessons for both of us; we have both learned what the value of human life is all about.

I have also learned from my wife Patty, that the choices we make, on a day by day situation, can bring healing to our bodies, to our minds and to our souls. My wife Patty asked that I make sure to write from my heart in a loving and humble manner the next few paragraphs which contained some very controversial subjects. I am now being called to say this again, as I did regarding Joe Paterno's life changing decision: All of us are called to make judgments moment by moment; we need to be aware that the harder the decision is to make the more we should reach out for God's help with our prayers. We do not want to make the wrong decision when the love for our brothers and sisters is involved in our decision, especially for the helpless ones. I need to make clear to you that what I will be writing in the next few paragraphs is written with love for all, **but especially for those who are being excluded and marginalize from our love because they do not look like us or are able to act like us.**

I would like to suggest to those of us who are parents, especially all mothers, to look into your hearts and ask yourself these questions: Did my little Suzie's or my little Johnny's life really only began after he or she was born? Why is it that we then worried so much about making sure we ate the right foods, we did not drink too much, or smoked, or take the wrong drugs while pregnant with our child? Could it be that we knew in our hearts that when our doctor told us that our actions were going to affect the development of our child's new life that it was not so much our bodies we would be harming, but our baby's body? We did not doubt that after we conceived little Johnny or little Suzie they were no longer just a part of our body, did we? Could it be that we knew that a unique other person was now completely dependent on our actions to develop in a normal way? We knew – and we did not have to take it on faith – that if we wanted our baby to grow up to be a normal healthy unique precious human being we were going to have to take good care of our bodies just as soon as we found out we were pregnant; that little Johnny or little Suzie's entire future was now totally dependent on our actions. As Daniel Patrick once said: "Everyone is entitled to his own opinion, but not to his own facts." When did any of us who are now parents start nurturing our new baby? Was it only after your little Johnny or your little Suzie was born? Or was it from the time you found out your child had been conceived and was starting their own life journey? If you have not experienced being a parent, ask your parents, or friends and family who are parents. Ask them, but do not tell them why you are asking the questions. In this manner you will know the answers came from their heart and not from any agenda regarding when life begins.

There are some of us who refuse to admit, what science has now proven beyond a reasonable doubt, that all individual human life begins at conception, just as many of us used to believe that the earth was flat because it appeared to be flat. The fact that a fetus does not appear to be just like a grown human does not change the fact that it is separate and unique human life at the beginning stage of that individual human life. Just because some of us do not want to believe that from conception forward what is developing and growing inside of a woman's body is a separate and unique human life does not change the fact that it is in fact a separate and unique human life. Some believed the earth was flat because it appeared to be flat, but that did not make it flat; the earth has always been round, and human life has always begun at conception.

My wife and I lost a baby through a miscarriage, and we both mourned her, we felt it was going to be the little girl we had wanted, but never had; my wife was able to get pregnant not too long afterward, and we had our second of our three sons . And although we are very happy and love our second son, and had my wife not had the miscarriage we would not have had our second son because she got pregnant not too long after her miscarriage, we will always know that we did have a little girl, but we were just not meant to have her grow up with us. It is with love and humility I would like to suggest that allowing a unique human life to continue to live should overrule the privacy of anyone of us because ending a unique human life that has only just begun is a choice that we should only make if another human life is in danger. If the woman ends her pregnancy and later has fifteen more children, none of them would be the one whose life was ended. It cannot be "ok" to end the life of one of God's children except to save the life of another one of God's children. There would be a great amount of love in the action of choosing to risk dying to save another human life, but it is a choice to be made only by the person whose life might possibly end to save that other human life. The rest of us should respect the life of all **"created in God's image"** (Genesis 1:27). You can't choose one human life over the other unless not making the choice will only allow both lives to end. You would then make the choice based on the greater chance of saving one life over the other – but only if neither person is able to respond to the question: "which of you should we try to save?"

Why do some of us want to say, what science has now otherwise proven beyond a reasonable doubt, that we are not a unique, one of a kind human life, until we are no longer dependent on our mother's body, and are born into the world? Our current knowledge of science tells us otherwise. To be born into the world is just another stage in our human life. Our current knowledge of science tells us that what makes us a unique individual began at conception. Again, Daniel Patrick once said: "Everyone is entitled to his own opinion, but not to his own facts." You could just as well say that our human life began at puberty because that is when we stopped being children and began to be adults with the ability to reproduce more human life, and saying this would also be wrong, and not based on any fact.

Over twenty years ago I wrote the following, speaking from the perspective of an unborn child:

> Who is growing inside of you Mother?
>
> Is it you or is it me, or am I a what?
>
> The genetic code in my cells is unique, but what does that mean?
>
> I am growing, but I am not complete. Won't you please let me be me?
>
> I cannot survive outside of you. I cannot speak.
>
> Why should you worry? You must be free. Is that it?
>
> I am a chain that binds you?
>
> If you recognize me as a separate individual person, you cannot be as free?
>
> Oh please mother I didn't ask to be.
>
> Ah, but you didn't ask for me either, that is something I have to be able to see.

Besides, I am not me; I have to be a what.

If I am me, you just can't be as free. A what, is easier to get rid of and deal with, than a me?

God knows who is growing inside of you...

Mother it is me!

I personally wish that the pro-choice argument that life does not begin until birth was correct because women have been oppressed and marginalized by some of the very people who sanctimoniously preach the pro-life argument of how human life is sacred, and yet at the same time are pro-death sentences. Most civilized countries in the world now abhor the death sentence option, and more and more states in our country are also now repealing the death sentence option in favor of life sentences without parole. And a few of these "pro-life" people will even somehow justify killing those who perform abortions, and they are not many, thank God; but how crazy is that?. However, "Everyone is entitled to his own opinion, but not to his own facts" (Daniel Patrick).

My son Marc, the one who made the movie called "Moving On" which I would like to share with you, made another movie about a person who could go back in time by pushing a button and then get to re-do anything he wanted to re-do. So I asked him to imagine that someone had invented a camera that could take pictures back in time of each one of us. In 2014 Marc was thirty-five years old, so I told him: "The camera is taking your picture from fifteen years ago when you were twenty years old, and there you are, one and only Marc. Then the camera is taking your picture when you were ten years old, and there you are, one and only Marc. Then the camera is taking your picture when you were four years old, and there you are, one and only Marc. Then the camera is taking your picture when you were first born, and there you are, one and only Marc. Then the camera is taking your picture when you were inside your Mother and you were six months after being conceived, and there you are, one and only Marc. Then the camera is taking your picture when you were only one week after being conceived, and there you are, one and only Marc. Then the camera is taking your picture, when you Marc first started your life inside your Mother, and there you are, one and only Marc. Finally, the camera is taking the picture right before you were conceived, and there you are not Marc, only a potential one and only Marc." I told him that as he went back in time those pictures of Marc started to look, less and less like the year 2014 one and only Marc, but they were all pictures of him none of the less, weren't they?

My brothers and sisters, **I believe liberty is our God-given right. It is our God-given right to choose love or to choose not to do so**; an important part of my message is that choosing love is always in your own best interest, but it is your God-given right. However, your right to swing your fist stops where another one of your brother or sister's nose begins. **And your right to privacy also stops where another one of your brother or sister's life begins!**

The "Golden rule," to do unto others as you would wish to be done unto you, should especially be applied where another unique, but completely dependent and helpless human life began. There is the argument that because a baby is completely dependent on his mother for life until being born, and doesn't yet completely look like us, it should therefore not be considered to be fully human; **this should not ring true to those of us who feel the helpless should always be protected whether they look different than us or not**. And this is just not based on any current scientific knowledge or fact. Another argument used to keep abortion legal is that people are going to do it anyway, so we should make it safer to do it. I humbly and respectfully suggest that God's call for us to love is asking us to put into place options for those desperate women, other than ending a unique human life; we need to give those who would choose to terminate their pregnancy help in dealing with their personal problems that does not involve ending a unique human life unless their own life is at risk. Science should continue to do research on human incubators, and or, transplanting the human fetus to a mother who cannot conceive, but otherwise is capable of having a baby. When science becomes able to terminate a pregnancy without also terminating the life of the unborn child, it will then give those who did not want to be pregnant the option for terminating their pregnancy, without also terminating the separate and unique human life now starting their own life journey. There is bonding and nurturing interaction going on between the growing unique human life inside of a pregnant woman and the mother to be well before the child is born, and to some degree with the father to be of the child. How could it be otherwise when even after many years have passed, parents who lost a child through a miscarriage still mourn the life of the unique person they lost? Infertile parents trying to conceive their own baby know how precious human life truly is, and they also know that conception is when human life begins. It was a very strong message that I received the other day: **What part of loving all your brothers and sisters is it that we do not understand?** However, I want to add that I was also guided, but not as directly as what I just mentioned above, that we have to forgive and love ourselves to also to be able to forgive and love others. Pope Francis is receiving the same message, "Every Person Matters." Please choose to love for your own sake, because it is always your choice, and that is the choice that will always matter to you. **God is love, and when we decide to love we are using love as a bridge to connect us to God and to each other.**

There are some of us that will agree with what I have just written regarding when human life begins, but will be in total disagreement with what I will now be writing. It is with love and humility that I would like both of those who agree with what I just wrote in my previous paragraphs, and those who disagree, and then those who will agree or disagree with what I will be writing in the following paragraph to open up your hearts to God's love. Both of these thoughts were written in complete love for God and for all of my brothers and sisters. Please open up your hearts and make the choice based on love for one another because deciding to love is always for your own best interest, and know that where there is love there will be God. Those who you disagree with are not always going to be wrong, and you are also not always going to be right. However, if you open your heart and make your decision based on love, God will be with you; and if you find the decision hard to make you should remember to pray for God's help; God will be there for you. It is God's will for us to do, on earth as it is in heaven, to love all of our brothers and sisters, whether they have already been born, or are still growing inside of their mothers' womb. However, the "Golden Rule" also calls us to love all of our brothers and sisters of a different sexual orientation as we would wish to be loved.

It is self-evident that people do not choose their sexual orientation. Why would you choose to be different than the majority, when that majority will make your life much harder for being a homosexual, than for being a heterosexual? This has been the situation for homosexuals throughout recorded history. You are called to love others for your own best interest, more so than for the good of those that you would choose to love. God has been asking us to treat others as we would wish to be treated, and it is not doing this simple request that continues to get mankind into trouble. Where there is love, there is God, and where there is no love, God is pushed out by those who decide not to love. So, yes, if you look into your hearts and see that your fellow brothers and sisters who are homosexual did not choose to be homosexual, and that God made them to be the way they are, then there is absolutely no way you can do anything other than to follow the Golden rule, to "do unto others as you would wish to be done unto you." I have known some very good people who were very loving and caring people, but were also homosexual. And all our brothers and sisters, no matter their sexual orientation, should be allowed to commit to each other in a loving and caring relationship without the rest of us making their ability to do so much harder than we would those who are heterosexual.

Churches who hold on to belief that one should treat homosexuals differently than anyone else should ask the four questions I previously mentioned to find out if the belief came from God: "Does the belief contradict that God's love is for everyone unconditionally?" "Does this belief call on us to do anything other than a loving act?" "Does it exclude any of our brothers and sisters?" "Does it ask us to do anything other than treat others as we would wish to be treated?" **The answers are yes to all four, not just one of the questions,** so why continue to hold to a belief that must not have come from God? Do the churches imagine homosexuals feel loved by those churches? Do the churches imagine that God wants them to exclude their brothers and sister whom God made to be homosexuals? Do the churches imagine that they are treating homosexuals the same way they would want to treated? **"Whatsoever you do to the least of your brothers that you do unto God"** (Matthew 25:45), so are homosexuals less than the least of your brothers?

The following are a couple e-mails I sent to a friend who told me we were not allowed to pick and choose from scripture what we wanted to believe:

> Gerald,
>
> Yes, we have to pick and choose what we believe; if any of the beliefs calls on us to choose other than love, we have to always choose love for our own best interest.
>
> It is by our love that we will truly be God's follower.
>
> We have the God-given right to choose love, and it will always be in our best interest to so choose.
>
> Have you ever met anyone who was always loving not bring peace and love to himself by choosing to love?
>
> I can think of many who bring conflict and misery to themselves when they choose not to be loving.
>
> We move closer to God when we choose love, but it is always our God-given right to choose.
>
> So, yes always pick and choose love to truly love God because

God is Love, and Hell is not.

Your friend,

Al Tamargo

Gerald,

As I mentioned to you, I am being inspired to write *God is Love, and Hell is not; a message of Love to All* – When we choose love we are choosing God" due to my daily prayers to be made into an instrument of God's love, but there was one instant early one Saturday morning, when as I was driving by myself on the way to play golf with a friend, that I actually received a very strong message that was almost a shout: "What part of loving all your brothers and sisters is it that we do not understand?" This message also had unimaginable love in it. Pope Francis is receiving the same message, "Every Person Matters."

So Gerald, please look at history and see all the many times religion has been used to justify breaking the "Golden Rule." It is why religion has always been part of the problem for mankind and not part of the solution. Slavery was justified by quoting scriptures; read your history, people actually did this!

However, if the four questions had been asked about those scriptures or anybody's belief to find out if they were relevant or if they came from God that were being used to justify slavery – religion would have been part of the solution and not part of the problem: "Does the belief contradict that God's love is for everyone unconditionally?" "Does this belief call on us to do anything other than a loving act?" "Does it exclude any of our brothers and sisters?" "Does it ask us to do anything other than treat others as we would wish to be treated?"

Yes Gerald, to be closer to God we have to always choose love, and when it comes to homosexuals all the answers are yes to all four of the questions, not just one of the questions. So why continue to hold to a belief that must not have come from God?

Following the "Golden Rule" will always bring you closer to God, breaking the "Golden Rule," not very much at all. **"What so ever you do to the least of your brothers and sisters that you do unto me."**

With sincere love and appreciation, your friend,

Al Tamargo

The following is my response to Liz, a relative who asked me to read *One Man One Woman, A Catholic's Guide to Defending Marriage* by Dale O'Leary:

Before I tell you my own thoughts regarding the book, I would like to tell you what happened to me the morning of this past Palm Sunday, March 29, 2015. My wife Patty woke me up when she came to bed around three am, and as it has happened before while writing my spiritual writing, these thoughts came to me that I thought were important to the subject of the book I have been writing: What makes sex holy is love. If there is no committed love the "Golden Rule" is being broken. One is only using the other without caring or without loving. Menopausal couples, or infertile couples can and do have sex that is holy. Sex without love, even within a traditional marriage of a man and a woman loses its holiness if it is used without love. Where there is love, there you will always find God. And then, after writing those thoughts I went back to sleep.

The next morning when I woke up, around 7:30 am that Palm Sunday, I picked up O'Leary's book and continued reading where I had left off. The following is what I read:

> In 1960, as a young Polish bishop named Karol Wojtyla, the future Pope John Paul II wrote a book called Love and Responsibility,

> in which he examined in detail the ideology that makes sexual pleasure the highest good. By reducing other persons to means for one's own enjoyment, this sexual "utilitarianism," he said, contradicts the fundamental law of love: "You shall love your neighbor as yourself," a corollary of which must be, "You shall not use your neighbor as an object." Although Sexual Utilitarianism may sound harmless and even quite appealing – everyone free to enjoy sexual pleasure! – it always ends with one person using another as an object. This is inconsistent with love and with human dignity.

As I read a mirror image of what I had written earlier that morning, I became emotional, feeling that all of humanity is like the *Prodigal Son* (Luke 15:11-32); the son who was not truly worthy of the unconditional love of his father. It took the *Prodigal Son* much hardship, brought on by his own actions, before he understood a small portion of the love the father had for him.

Regarding what Dale O'Leary tells us in her book, *One Man One Woman*, the following is what I got from it: Dale O'Leary, like many loving caring people who truly want to follow God's call to be loving to the least of their brothers and sisters is missing the substance of just what it is all of us are being called by God to do. It is why I know I have been inspired by God to ask all my brothers and sisters to ask the four questions regarding whatever their own beliefs are: Does the belief contradict that God's love is for everyone unconditionally? Does this belief call on us to do anything other than a loving act? Does it exclude any of our brothers and sisters? Does it ask us to do anything other than treat others as we would wish to be treated?

O'Leary tells us that if we give in on one of our beliefs we might lose out on others. She mentions "The Pro Life movement" as an example of what could go by the wayside, if people give in and allow homosexuals to commit to each other in a loving relationship society calls marriage. However, if you ask the four questions about defending the helpless unborn individuals we see the belief is no, it does not contradict that God's love is for everyone unconditionally, it is including the individual unborn human life. No, it does not call on us to do anything other than a loving act; it does the opposite, you are defending the helpless. No, it does not exclude any of our brothers and sisters; it includes the unborn as our brothers and sisters. And finally, no, it does not call on us to do anything other than treat others as we would wish to be treated.

Again, "If you are hungry and you find a small stone in your bowl of cereal, you do not take the whole bowl of cereal and dump it on the ground, you go ahead and pick the stone out of your bowl, and then eat the cereal in your bowl" (My son Marc's meditating retreat).

"The Sermon on the Mount"

I tell you, you must love those who you have learnt to think as you enemies, and if they oppress you, you must pray for them. So shall you be like God your Father; you know He makes his sun to shine on bad and good alike, and send his rain upon all men, whether they obey or disobey his will. Supposing that you love only those that love you back, there is no special merit in that, is there? Quite disreputable people rival you there! **Or if you are friendly only with people of your own set,** that implies nothing more than average good nature; the very heathen are equal to that! **No you are to be God's men; your love is to be as catholic as His.**

O'Leary and those who want to "Defend Marriage" believe that it is the "how" one expresses love to another that is the substance of what makes love "Holy." However, the substance of what makes love "Holy" is the "Intentions of the "What" in expressing love. Suppose, one or both, of a heterosexual couple was handicapped and the only way for them to show their love for each other was the "how" of how the homosexual couples do. Is the "how" the substance of their love? Or is it the "intentions of the "what"? The intentions of their "what" is self-evident the substance of their love and will always be universal, today or a million years from now. It will not matter if mankind goes out into the universe and discovers other intelligent life forms who reproduce by using four different sex types, the "what" will stand, the "how" not so much.

O'Leary spent a lot of time arguing that homosexuals are not born that way, but become that way. And I would argue, what difference does that really make? Would it make any difference if the handicapped person was born handicapped, or became handicapped later in life? They did not choose to be handicapped. O'Leary would argue that all homosexual can change their inclination and attraction for people of the same sex. And while that may be true for some who could have gone either way, it is not true for the majority of our brothers and sisters who are homosexuals. And again, what is the substance of a committed relationship? Is it the "how"? Or is it the "intentions" of the "what"?

What makes sex holy is the love expressed by the sexual actions; the giving and receiving that are two sides of the same coin, love. Without love sex is not holy because it is not connecting with (God) love. Sex without love is empty pleasure that does not really satisfy the soul.

There was one thing, regarding how homosexuals who want to adopt are treated that I totally agree with her, and that is when it comes to adopting children. But then, it is no longer about the homosexual we are really talking about. We are talking about innocent children and what would be in their best interest. So, yes, I agree that children are better off when placed in a loving home that has both a father and mother, if everything else is equal, because they will experience the diversity of the love of a mother and father. And therefore, if everything else is equal, preference should be given to them. Only when the only choice is a single parent or an orphanage would it be in the best interest of the child to have a loving homosexual couple adopt them. Diversity, by the way, is why we should want to have all institutions integrated so that man, woman, or homosexual have equal opportunity for leadership roles.

Finally, let us ask the four questions about the belief that homosexuals should be excluded from committing to each other in a loving marriage. Does the belief contradict that God's love is for everyone unconditionally? Yes it kind of does, because we are saying the love that they want to commit to each other is not worthy in the light of God. Does this belief call on us to do anything other than a loving act? Yes, it does, because love is being denied to those who want to commit their love to each other. Does it exclude any of our brothers and sisters? Yes, without a doubt we are excluding all our brothers and sisters who are homosexuals by not allowing them to commit to each other in loving relationship. Does it ask us to do anything other than treat others as we would wish to be treated? Again, yes, it is for sure asking us to do other than treat homosexuals the way those of us who are heterosexual would treat one another.

Toward the end of her book O'Leary almost gets it when she said, "Real love means wanting what is best for another person, and what is best for persons with SSA is that they find the love they need, the freedom they've been denied." However, she then went on to say: "we won't be swayed when they claim that if we really loved them, we would give in to their demands. It's precisely because we really love them that we won't."

O'Leary talked about a slippery slope if we give in on one thing, but the way I see it if all religions started asking those four questions about any of their beliefs, the only slippery slope answering those question in the negative will take us to is **"God's will on earth as it is in heaven"** (Matthew 6:10). Where there is love, there you will always find God. There was one very strong message I received while doing my spiritual writing that was almost a shout: "What part of loving all your brothers and sisters is it that we do not understand?" This message also had unimaginable love in it.

I also responded to Liz's response to my e-mail with the following:

> You avoided the issue which is the core and substance of two

loving individuals who want to commit to love each other until death do them part who are being denied the ability to do so, and that you and so many others call it "sin" against God. However Liz, **where there is love there you will always find God and not sin.** Christ said "it is by you love they will know you are my disciples." And there is no love in denying two people, who want to commit to love each other until death do them part, from doing so. Liz, Hell is the opposite of God's love. Where there is love you will always find God, because God is love. **And sin is the opposite of love, there can't be any sin where there is true love.**

This will be my last two additions to my correspondence with Liz, but I made additional points I like to share with you:

I know that you and many others truly feel you are following God's will for us on earth as it is in heaven. But, do you truly believe that the "how" we love each other is going to matter in heaven? Again, that the way we reproduce in the spec in the universe that we call planet earth is the only way God created every living intelligent being in the infinite universe?

However, Christ did say to us that it was by our love that everyone would know we were his disciples. And as I told Manuel in our e-mail correspondence on this subject: The point is that it really doesn't matter if they are born that way or become that way for whatever reason, the fact is that they are the way they are. So the "Golden Rule" should apply for them, and to say that their wanting to commit to each other in a loving relationship until death do them part is against what God wants? God is love, so where is the love we are called to have for others? The action of preventing others from committing to each other just doesn't seem to go along with what we are called to do, which is to treat others as we would wish to be treated. It just sounds like more of the same stuff that people have used to excuse not treating others as we would wish to be treated.

And I have said it about people that do not have empathy for others, that they live in their own little world, well it seems as if we act like the earth is the center of the universe, and we know better, or we should. But do we act like the earth is just a spec in the universe and that what we currently know is almost nothing compared to all that there is for us to learn?

Again, the core of the issue is love. The "how" is not the substance of love it is "the intentions of the what" that matter in how we love one another. You say: "It is their choice to live a life of chastity or have a relationship with someone from their same sex." How is it that you can call on them to only have those two choices when it comes to their wanting to commit to "till death do us part" loving relationship with someone else, and yet say you are doing a loving act toward them; that you are treating them the same way you would want to be treated. Do you give heterosexual couples the same choice? You and others who want to "Defend Marriage" do not see that the "how" can't be important because it is not universal, the "intentions of the what" will always be universal and is what matters to the God who has created an infinity universe of which mankind only has a hint and very little knowledge. That is the second of my three very important core messages: The second is that all of us need to be humble and accept that mankind's spiritual journey has only just begun. Believing that we already have all the answers is good portion of the intolerance we have for one another, and not focusing on the substance of what God's will for us truly is, we are to choose love. Again, **"it is by your love for one another they will know you are my disciples"** (John 13:35).

Much love and appreciation, but know Liz that truly treating others as we would wish to be treated will always be "God's will for us on earth as it is in heaven." There is no way that preventing two people from committing to love each other "until death do you part" or do so only in "chastity" is treating homosexuals the same as we treat heterosexuals. Again, where is the love for those who have the "same sex attraction"?

We are saying to them: it matters to us, so it should matter to you, and the "how" you love each other is just not acceptable to us; when the "how," absolutely in the case of those who want to commit to love each other "until death do them part," is only an expression of their love and not evil in any way. The intentions of the what, is what is important, whether homosexual or heterosexual.

With true love, as I mentioned in "To be powerful, giving and receiving should be two sides of the same coin, love.," the love intention has to be humble and not selfish, and what is important no matter what your sexual inclination might be. But again, to be true love, you can't allow your love to hurt or do harm anyone else in the "how" it is expressed. You can't have true love for one person if by your actions you hurt another – who is also loved by God.

Christians especially should remember Jesus' words: **"it is by your love for one another, that everyone will recognize you as my disciples, if you have love for one another**" (John 13:34 – 35). Did Christ ask us to exclude any of our brothers and sisters from our love? **"It is by your love for one another, that everyone will recognize you as my disciples, if you have love for one another"** (John 13:34 – 35) – not by calling yourself Christians! God is asking all of mankind – and not just those who call themselves Christians – to not only talk the talk of love, but walk the walk of love!"

Chapter 5

Churches' Traditions can Sometimes Move Us Away from God

Please decide to love for your own sake, because it is always your choice, and that is the choice that will always matter to you. **God is love, and when we decide to love we are using love as a bridge to connect us to God and to each other.**

Again, much of what is getting mankind into trouble is the belief that there is not much we need to learn spiritually, and that all of our religious traditions have all the answers we will ever need.

What we need to do is make sure we start to focus on the substance of what God's will is for us, and make sure we are answering the four questions about our belief correctly.

If a church tradition is contradicting God's call on us to be as catholic with our love as God is with his, then it is with love and humility that I would like to suggest that some of the churches might want to consider that denying the world of the full spiritual gifts that some of us have to offer who happen to not want to be celibate, or have been made by God to be homosexual, or to be female, is terminating a spiritual path which might contribute much love and understanding to the rest of us; a tradition that excludes some of us from achieving our full spiritual potential **"can't be OK" either**. Just because when the tradition was started society was not ready to accept women as equals or homosexuals as equals is no reason to continue it when we now should know better. It is with love, respect and humility I would like to suggest that excluding anyone from being instruments of God's love is not a loving decision; to exclude anyone who wants to be an instrument of God's love by some of us who have already so chosen, is not a loving act to the rest of us who might benefit from the God-given gift those persons are choosing to share with the rest of us. **Why**

do we then complain that there are not enough of us choosing to be instrument of God's love to take care of the spiritual needs of the rest of us?

It is with love and humility that I would like to suggest that God's love is for all, and that God wants you to help and encourage all of his children who want to be instruments of his love and peace to achieve their full potential. When you exclude some of us who are choosing to be instruments of God's love from following their vocation, you are excluding others from giving the full love God would like for you to receive through those instruments. You are moving yourself away from God's love, and doing so is not in your best interest. Where there is love, there is God.

I would like to ask you to reflect on the fact that the societies that embrace diversity, not only grow stronger, but also enjoy more peace and joy. Every person matters is the message God wants you to embrace. Our differences contribute unique talents. Why would you exclude some of your brothers and sisters from following their full vocation, and deprive our society from the gifts God would like for us to receive?

When you exclude those who want to follow God's calling from their vocation, it is like what a city would do if they were to dam their main source of water (God) and prevent most of the water from getting to their city. They are diverting most of the water from getting to their city, and then why would they then complain? "We do not have enough water to meet the needs of the people in our city." Well stop diverting the water!

One day there will be a woman Pope, and the United States will also have a woman President, just like we finally have a black President. **It will happen!** Why is it I am so certain that these things will happen? The reason I am so certain that these things will happen is because there is no reason for anyone of us to be excluded from being God's instrument of his love – only our prejudice. Many of us who pray to God are getting very strong messages from God; I received the message: **What part of loving all your brothers and sisters is it that we do not understand? And Pope Francis is receiving the same message, "Every Person Matters."** Most of the people who are doing the excluding are good people who pray to God all the time but do not yet understand what it is that they are doing: God is answering our prayers and we will come to know that when we exclude some of us who are choosing to be instruments of God's love from following their vocations, we are excluding ourselves from the love God would like for us to receive through those instruments; we are moving ourselves away from God's love, and doing so is not in our best interest. Where there is love, there is God. **God is love, and when we decide to love we are using love as a bridge to connect us to God and to each other.**

Why is it that love connects us to God and to each other? I know many of you will be able to think of many instances where reaching out with love to someone else has created harmony and happiness, but I will give some everyday examples from my own experiences: One is when one of my sisters wrote me an e-mail blasting me for what she thought I was trying to do when I had copied her on an e-mail I had sent to someone else in our family. But rather than blasting back at her in my response, I asked for her forgiveness if my words had hurt her in anyway, and I told her how much I loved her and I appreciated her for all the good things I see in her; her next responding e-mail was full of love right back at me, which was a win, win, for both of us.

I would like to offer you an additional everyday example of love in action from one of my own personal experiences. When a very good friend and I were playing golf one day, and he thought I was minimizing his knowledge of the game he told me that if I was not going to listen to him he did not want anything more to do with me. He was going to go home. I immediately responded with my own heartfelt appreciation for him as a person and as a friend. He calmed down and forgave me and then we were able to enjoy playing the rest of the game.

I also want to offer another everyday example from my own experience where I did not make the right choice. I do not want anyone to think that I always make the right choices. I was trying to explain to one of my other sisters my thoughts regarding God not sending anyone to hell, but that it is us that send ourselves there. But my sister kept interrupting me; she wanted to tell me her own thoughts about God not only loving us, but also having to be a just God. To my shame, I lost my temper and told her to please let me finish my thoughts. I missed out on a chance to demonstrate my love for her, and thereby keep our own line of communication with God's love and peace open. Being a loving person works at least as much for those who give it as it does for those who receive it.

The following came to me the morning after the incident with my sister, where I lost my temper. Her concern, which she kept trying to express to me when she interrupted me several times, regarding God not only being a loving God but also a just God, had been answered by Pope Francis. Pope Francis had just recently communicated to us a message from God, when talking about homosexual priests: "who am I to judge." God was communicating to us, through Pope Francis, God does not judge us, but only loves us unconditionally. That it is ourselves who decide whether to move closer to the light of his love for us on earth right now, and after our death. God's love is truly more like what a father's love would be for us on earth, rather than what a judge's would be for us. What father's love would condemn a son or a daughter to eternal punishment? God is love, and it is you who by making the wrong decisions create your own misery when you move away from the light of his love.

Pope Francis wrote in his book *The Church of Mercy* published in 2014 the following in which he expresses the same thought I was communicating to my sister in 2013:

> In the Church, the God we encounter is not a merciless judge but is like the Father in the Gospel parable. You may be like the son who left home, who sank to the depths, farthest from the Gospel.

> When you have the strength to say, "I want to come home," you will find the door open. God will come to meet you because he is always waiting for you – God is always waiting for you. God embraces you, kisses you, and celebrates. That is how the Lord is, that is how the tenderness of our heavenly Father is.

Yet in an article published in the Catholic Review for the Archdiocese of Baltimore, published for December 2015, Bishop Robert Barron an Auxiliary bishop of the Archdiocese of Los Angeles and founder of Word on Fire Catholic Ministries said the following about Pope Francis' emphasis on God's mercy:

> In order to clear things up, a little theologizing is in order. It is not correct to say that God's essential attribute is mercy. Rather, **God's essential attribute is love,** since love is what obtains among the three divine person from all eternity. **Mercy is what love looks like when it turns toward the sinner.** To say that mercy belongs to the very nature of God, therefore, would be to imply that sin exists within God himself, which is absurd.

I respectfully have highlighted the two things that bishop Robert Barron said in his article that are right on, and do not contradict God's unconditional love for us. But then he went on to say: "To say that mercy belongs to the very nature of God, therefore, would be to imply that sin exists within God himself, which is absurd." And of course he is right that it would be absurd to say sin exists within God himself – but not to say it is within our choice. **Sin is the opposite of love, and therefore the opposite of God himself!**

> Again: "It takes two to love. It takes liberty. It takes the right to reject. If there were no hell, we would be like the animals. No hell, no dignity."
>
> – Flannery O'Connor, 1959

Pope Francis' message is also not a new message God has been sending to us; I was looking through some of the books my wife has on her book shelf shortly after I wrote the preceding paragraph, and I was drawn to look at the following book. The book was, *How to Meditate* by Lawrence Le Shan. In it Le Shan made the following dedication: "To Max Grossman, who taught me that **the opposite of 'injustice' is not 'justice', but 'love'."** This Lawrence Le Shan book was published in 1974. I have highlighted the above part of Le Shan dedication because it resonated so much with my own thoughts on what true justice means. It resonates with Jesus Christ's messages of love to you, doesn't it?

The next night, after I wrote the above mentioned quote from Le Shan's book, it came to me that the reason the quote resonated with me is that those who do "injustice" are choosing not to love; so for us to bring true justice to the world, the justice we bring to those who chose not to love has to be given to them with love. Those who decide not to love need love more – they are totally missing it – they need our love and our prayers. However, we do not allow injustice to go on, we have to always protect ourselves and other innocents – but to be true justice when we give justice we should pray that those who have done the injustice will find their way home to love. Love is a choice each of us should always make because it brings us closer to God.

The next morning after writing the preceding paragraph, it came to me while working out: Unconditional love is the choice God wants all of his children to make, but not force us to make. You should always try to be instruments of God's love – for your own best interest. Those who need to learn that they are not going to be bring happiness to anyone with their decision not to love – including themselves – need your good example much more than anyone else. They need your help to see by the peace and joy you are receiving with your decision to love – that it is in their best interest when they decide to love. Forced love would not be true love; love is a choice we each have to make. You can only pray for God's help when your brothers and sisters are making it hard for you to love them by their choice not to love. **However, you especially need to pray for God's help – on a moment by moment love decision – to make sure it is**

not you who is making it hard for your other brothers and sisters to love you. You need to make sure – whether intentionally or unintentionally – you are not making it hard for others to love you. And therefore, by all mean atone for your misdeeds to your brothers and sisters to make it easier for them to love you back – and for you to forgive yourself. **But no atonement to God is ever needed by you, or anyone else. God is unconditional Love for all.**

This message came to me, regarding what we are failing to understand about God's love for all of us. That when we decide not to love our brothers and sisters it is not God who is judging us as having failed God, **it is those who choose not to love their brothers and sisters who are failing themselves.** God loves all of us so when we decide to love another, we love God. And when you decide not to love another you move yourselves from the light of God's love. It is like a parent who has one of the sons or daughters doing harm to one of his brothers or sisters; the parent does not stop loving the one doing the harm, or the one being harmed. However, the one doing the harm to his brother or sister is moving himself away from the parent's love. The parent loves all of the sons or daughters equally. The one doing the harm is not only creating harm to his brother or sister, but also to himself. The parent would want the other brothers and sisters to prevent the one doing the harm from harming anyone, including himself, but not for anyone to stop loving him. The parent still loves all the sons or daughters unconditionally. Deciding to love creates happiness and joy; deciding to hate brings misery to the one who does so.

Very few people who do evil things in this world are totally without love in their lives. They will love some members of their family, but not all. They will love most people of their own culture or race, but again, not all. They will love people with their own sexual orientation, and yes again, not all. And what absolutely should never ever be – because God is love – they will only love people with their own religious belief. And yes, even with people who hold their own religious belief, they will not love all.

What came to me one night as I reflected on Le Shan dedication: "To Max Grossman, who taught me that the opposite of 'injustice' is not 'justice', but 'love'" was that it would not be a contradiction to say that **the opposite of love is not "hate" or "injustice," but "Hell."** Hell is where you send yourself by choosing to move away from love: **God is love and Hell is not.**

One of the main reason religions are part of the problem and not part of the solution is not focusing on the substance of God's love, and instead focusing on the messengers God is using to help us. A friend, who I had not seen for many years, and I were catching up on what we have been doing and I mentioned that I was in the process of writing a spiritual book. I mentioned to him some of my thoughts regarding how mankind believing that any one of us, or group of us, has all the answers about an infinite God, is what is keeping us from growing and creating conflict rather than love in the world. He asked me to read a very good book called "More than a Carpenter" by Josh McDowell. After I left his office I immediately went to the local book store and bought the book. What is striking me about the book is how McDowell – like many Christians – is focusing on Christ as the important reason God sent him to us rather than on the message Christ wanted to teach us. Where there is love there is God. We are not getting it – God has unconditional love for all of us with no exception or exclusions. The message of love God has been sending mankind is what we still do not seem to get.

Unfortunately, too many of us still do not get it. You need to protect yourselves and the innocent from those who would harm you, but not stop loving them. I am reminded of an incident that happened some years ago: My wife Patty and I owned, what has been to this point, the most loving and cuddly dog with everyone in our family. But one day, when I was not careful in making sure I kept the door from our house to the garage closed, when the garage door was opened – that loving dog ran out of our house and chased after a very nice lady who just happened to be jogging in front of our house and bit her on the leg. I learned that day that one has to deal with what is in this world, not what we wished it would be. Our dog was a loving dog toward us, but it was in her nature to also be protective of her territory. I did not stop loving that dog, but I was much more careful how I handled her going forward. She showed me her nature; she was loving toward some, but not all. Too many of us have not learned that God's will for us, on earth as it is in heaven, is to love all of our brothers and sisters with no exceptions or exclusions. **We are just not there yet!** So we need to protect ourselves and the innocent from those who do not yet understand. But forgive, continue to pray, and love those who have yet to realize it is in their own best interest not to exclude anyone from their love. **To forgive those who do not yet understand what they are doing; this is the message Jesus Christ gave to us as he was dying on the cross (Luke23:24).**

When Christ died on the cross to show us a better way, he did this for us to learn from his example of love. When as he was dying he said, **"forgive them because they do not know what they are doing,"** he was talking to us – not God – because forgiveness is always included in God's unconditional love. God does not need to forgive any of us because he loves us all unconditionally, whether we are saints or sinners. It is all of us who need to forgive our brothers and sisters who are not as advanced in their own spiritual path and have yet to realize that love is for their own best interest – right here and right now. **Your choice to love will bring you closer to God, and give you peace and joy, and then will also continue to do this later when you die.** Again, please pray for them to join you in your choice to love, and also for yourself, so than you don't join them in their choice not to love. It is always your choice, not God's. **God chose to love us first** (John 4:19).

You move closer to God's light of love when you decide to love, because God loves all. **God is love, and when we decide to love we are using love as a bridge to connect us to God and to each other.**

It is a moment by moment decision we are called to make, and making the right decision is for our own best interest and good.

The next time I find myself getting ready to lose my temper I have promised myself that I will take a deep breath, and exhale, and then pray for God's help, with the full knowledge that just by choosing to pray, rather than losing my temper opens the line of communication to the love God wants to send to all of us, but that we need to choose and want; God will not force you to love because he created you in his image, with the ability to decide, and not be programed to love. Ask and you will receive. These are principles that will work for you in all phases of your life, including how you conduct businesses.

Chapter 6

God's Love Principles Work in Business – when we let them

I have noticed in my forty-four years of business experience that excellent businesses try to solve their customers' problems and demonstrate by their actions that they care. When they do this, it allows those customers to see that it is not about just trying to get money from them. It is also about building a long term trusting relationship with them. It can be a win, win, for both parties. Sometimes customers are unreasonable, but excellent companies will try to accommodate them anyway, and it pays off. In addition, these excellent companies will treat their employees fairly, and it is not just a "good" thing for them to do, but also very good business, because those employees will go the extra mile for the customers of their employers. So the really excellent companies know it is really, win, win, and win for all three parties, owners, employees, and customers: It starts with the owners of the company deciding they want to prosper by providing the most value to all who are involved in giving as well as receiving those products and services.

What many businesses do not seem to understand is that loyalty is a two way street; all business want their customers and their employees to be loyal to them, but fail to do their part in making it a win, win, for everybody involved and thereby end up losing the loyalty of customers and employees. Any business who loses the loyalty of their employees, and or, of their customers, has forgotten that loyalty is a two way street. Excellent companies have a culture of win, win, for everyone involved with them and it is ingrained in how they go about doing their day to day business to celebrate and appreciate the loyalty of both their employees and their customers by doing the things for them which will earn that loyalty.

I will never forget, way back in 1971, when I started working in the paint industry for Duron Paint Company, there was a man in his seventies named Chuck who had started working for Duron when it first got started in 1949. Chuck had to retire because his health was not allowing him to work full time any longer. At that time Duron did not have a formal retirement program; it was two years later before a retirement program was started. Duron told Chuck that he could work part time three days per week, but not to worry about his pay if he did not feel well enough to come in, because Duron was not going to forget all the work he had done to bring Duron to where they were at that time. Duron earned the loyalty of a twenty-two-year-old employee at that time named Al Tamargo who saw a company who cared about loyalty being a two way street.

I have always said that loyalty has to go both ways and has to be earned, but it can be lost over a period of time – if one of the parties starts to take the other party for granted. This is true for any relationship, whether it is personal or business.

There was a change in the top management of the company, but it took seven years of me having increases in my sales territory, but decreases in my W2 pay, before I found no alternative but to look for greener pastures.

It is a shame that the owners who had taken charge of the company lost sight of what it was that had created that Duron "magic." It was never D – U – R – O – N, it was the people who cared so much about people and wanted to treat others as they would wish to be treated. There were still many people in the company with the "magic," but the top management did not get it – and old Chuck would have been out of luck with the people making the decisions by the time I left the company. Only the echo of the "Camelot" of the paint industry remained.

I was fortunate to have been a part of that "magic." We know it is very rare in this dog eat dog business world, and unfortunately even more rare to have it last – when people who do not realize what the "magic" is take over managing the company; this is why companies that have this "magic" are not easy to find. It wasn't too long after I left the company that Duron's owners sold the company to one of the major competitors with whom Duron used to compete. However, the "Camelot" of the paint industry had already been sold by then – only the echo of "Camelot" was sold to the competitor.

The really excellent businesses also see themselves as good stewards to the environment and to the service they owe to society at large and thereby become dominant in their industry because they attract the best employees, who in turn attract the most loyal customers, who in turn attract the most wise investors and owners to join the organization. These excellent companies, however, only stay excellent by being aware that, the minute you think you have it made, you don't. And although you can bank loyalty from your employees and customers to a certain extent, if you stop earning their loyalty it eventually runs out.

I would like to share with you a quote from Pope Francis in his address to the Diplomatic Corps on January 14, 2014:

> I wish to mention another threat to peace, which arises from the greedy exploitation of environmental resources. Even if 'nature is at our disposition', all too often we do not 'respect it or consider it a gracious gift which we must care for and set at the service of our brothers and sisters, including future generations. Here too what is crucial is responsibility on the part of all in pursuing, in a spirit of fraternity, policies respectful of this earth which is our common home. I recall a popular saying: 'God always forgives, we sometimes forgive, but when nature – creation – is mistreated, she never forgives!'

You might argue that there are companies who seem to have achieved material success, but seem to only care about the bottom line profit of the company without also caring for their employees and customers. I would ask you to go out and meet the people who are involved with such companies, owners, employees and customers and find out how happy and satisfied are they with their association with such companies; have those companies earned the loyalty of their employees or their customers? At the end of the day, it is the companies who strive to win for everyone who deals with them, who will make it a pleasure and earn the loyalty of those who deal with them; those are the companies who will be around for the long term and have true success. The companies who live by the "Golden Rule" bring joy to everyone who comes into contact with them.

In addition, companies who only care about their own bottom line profit without realizing that very bottom line profit depends on the long term loyalty of their employees and customers, will not make the investments to keep themselves at the cutting edge of quality services and products for their industry. Accountants assigned a monetary value to the "good will" of a company for a very good down to earth reason; it pays to earn that "good will" to the bottom line profit of a company.

I want to offer you another personal example of how companies can earn or lose "good will." I recently had a situation with the investment company I have been doing business with for over thirty years, which can illustrate this fact. The company is mainly a mutual fund company, who also has an associated broker side for those of their customers who would also like to purchase individual stocks, bonds, or saving certificates from time to time. Due to the company being mainly a mutual funds company, their charges for doing trades is slightly more than double what a discount broker would charge. However, when it comes to large trades of over one thousand shares of stock, they also charge a percentage which can add up to hundreds of dollars if one of their customers wants to do a trade that involves large quantities of stock shares. I called them and explained that I was very happy with their excellent service and their response to my needs for over thirty years, but that I needed to do a one- time trade to move my position from seventeen thousand shares of one company, to be able to purchase fifteen thousand shares of another company with the proceeds from the sale of the seventeen thousand shares. I told them I did not mind paying slightly more than double to do trades with them because I did not need to do trades very often, but this one-time trade I wanted to do was going to cost me thirty times as much, and would they be willing to meet me half way; I told them about my feelings that loyalty should be a two way street, and that companies spend thousands of dollars, if not millions, in trying to gain new customers, why would they object to meeting a loyal customer on a one time basis to keep that loyalty? They told me about their policy charges, but then asked me what did I have in mind? I told them that because of their excellent service, and the fact that I would not be doing trades that frequently I really did not want to go elsewhere to do my business transaction, and that I would meet them half way on their charges, if they were willing to do so. They went ahead and accepted the deal, **and it was for sure a win, win for both of us.** That mutual fund company will probably keep my business for the rest of my life, and I will transfer both my current employer 401 K fund when I retire in the next couple years, and probably my wife's 401 K fund also, when it is time for her to retire. I won because on the day that we actually did the trade the company stocks that I was selling went up ten cents per share at the time we did the trade, and the company stocks I was buying stayed the same as it had closed the day before. However, the company stock I bought ended the day seven cents ahead of what I purchased the stocks at, and the company stocks I sold, which were ten cents ahead when I sold my shares ended the day at five cents for share less than what I had sold for. If my offer to meet them half way had not been accepted I would have lost much more than even the additional fees they were going to charge me, but they would have lost all of my future business. As I mentioned to them, when I was asking them to meet me half way; it was not about the money they were going to charge me, it was about my feeling that loyalty should be a two way street. Just on the purchase side of my trade, I gained $1,050, and on the sold side I would have lost $850, for a total net gain of $1,900.

Another example of how business can be – and should be, win,

win – came to me as I was trying to go back to sleep one night at the end of April, 2014; I had heard that the U.S Senate had not been able to pass a minimum wage bill; the argument used by those in opposition to the bill was that it was going to cost jobs, and those who were in favor of the bill argued that it was a matter of justice for anyone who worked a full time job to at least make enough money to be above the poverty level. What came to me was to ask those who argued that raising the minimum wage would cost jobs because companies would not be able to hire as many workers and still make a profit, is the following question: **How many jobs does it cost when the CEO of America's great companies make so many more multiples of what their workers make?**

An article in The Washington Post, by Harold Meyerson, discussed the same subject the next day, May 1, 2014. It was titled "A CEO tax on inequality." It talked about a committee of the California State Senate which had just recommended to the full Senate a bill that would cut the state taxes on companies with lower ratios between their chief executives' pay and the pay of their medium workers, and raise taxes on the kind of insanely high gap between the chief executive and medium worker pay. The article mentioned that, according to studies by the Economic Policy Institute, in 1965 the ratio between what the chief executive made and what their workers made was 20 to 1, but by 2012 it had risen to 273 to 1. Were the chief executives in 2012 that much better? Were the workers in 2012 that much worse?

It is a fact that the rich are getting richer, and the poor and the middle class are getting squeezed. **Yes, it is a matter of justice to have a fair living minimum wage – but also it is a win, win for everyone – even the rich.** The minimum wage needs to be there to protect all of the powerless because we know the people with power will always protect themselves. A minimum wage should be a living wage, **and most important it should be inflation adjusted or it will tend to go away.** The people with the power will always take care of themselves; **we need not worry about a minimum wage for the CEOs of the world!**

The thing that the politicians, and even the people with wealth are missing is the fact that what allows the rich to get richer is that the poor and the middle class have some buying power; **there might come a point – if the working poor and the middle class buying power continues to erode – that consumers will not be able to afford to buy as much, the rich will not be able to have as much real wealth. It is the people who work hard to produce and create new products that make all of us have more real wealth – not the idle rich.**

You should be able to see that one rich person can only consume so much; they can only buy a limited amount of houses, cars, computers, and so on. But the argument also goes that if the wealthy have more money they will create more jobs by investing the extra wealth in growing their businesses. But who is going to be able to afford the additional goods they would want to sell if everyone else has less disposable income? **Perhaps they would sell their goods to the middle class of other countries who are doing a better job of improving their middle class wealth?** However, if millions of workers have more disposable income, many more houses are going to be built, cars, computers, and so on. Trickle up economy works, but trickle down economy, not so much. It is always the greater numbers of people who can purchase the greater number of goods that will make the economy stronger for everyone. The few at the one percent of earnings are only able to purchase few goods by comparison. In addition, the motivation is much stronger for the people who are not rich to spend their earning to improve their lives, and their numbers are many, many more times than the rich. Everyone wins with trickle up economics – even the rich.

It is a win win for everyone, and we should not fall for the argument that having a strong minimum living wage, adjusted for inflation, will cost jobs. It will create more jobs in the long run because consumers will have more money to spend to improve their life. And yes, it will allow the rich to get even richer – but not at the expense of the rest of us – but by creating real wealth. **The law of supply and demand should be clear to everyone: if you have extra**

supply, but hardly anybody can afford it, the prices will go down until you decrease the supply. However, if you have more demand than there is supply because more people can now afford it – then the prices will go up until the wealthy see the opportunity to make more money and increase the supply and thereby make themselves wealthier. Everyone will win with the increase in demand. You can see it with countries like China becoming more of a world power as the purchasing power of their middle class has grown.

No country should want to export their goods because not enough of their own people can afford to purchase those goods – no matter what those good are. Whether it is cars, computers, cell phones, gasoline, or God forbid – food. The only reason countries should have for exporting their goods should be because they want to trade with other countries the goods for which there is so much supply that the people in their countries have more than enough of those goods – not because there are not enough of their own people who are able to afford buying those goods. And so all countries should want to trade for the goods other countries have excess supplies, and for which due to their excess supply they can afford to offer lower prices. **The more people who can afford to buy everyone's goods for less, the better the whole world will be – yes, even the wealthy.**

The argument that as wages grow it motivates companies to use more automation faster, and put workers out of work, will also not hold. Not if society sees the benefit of training and education for workers ahead of the automation curve. And there is also this, most of us humans prefer to deal with a caring human. Consider this: when you go out to eat, do you enjoy the experience more where you interact with a human? Or do you enjoy it more when you go to a fast food place and just get your food? I do not foresee humans being able to make machines who can choose to love us for many hundreds of years – if ever. Automation increases the supplies by increasing efficiency, and if demands drops because there are fewer workers who can afford the goods due to being out of work, the prices for the supply will drop. The law of supply and demand will also apply to the workers. The workers who remain working will be worth more money because there are fewer workers qualified to do the work that machines are still not able to do. Those workers without work will then be motivated to get the training and education to get into the sections of the work force that have more demand for workers than there are workers. We can continue to support the displaced workers by the automation to get new training and education, as we are already doing. Look at the track record of automation: Has it increased the overall quality of life? Or has it decreased it? It has increased it. Hasn't it? When Henry Ford started making cars in assembly lines, rather than one at the time – that was a good thing. Wasn't it?

The following is an e-mail I sent my brother Manuel Tamargo, who has strong Libertarian belief, but who will make exceptions when it comes to protecting the helpless:

> Manuel,
>
> The true wealth of this world and the next one is love. You are called to love your neighbor for a reason – it is in your best interest because when you decide to love it connects you with God – God is love.
>
> The answer of a just living wage is not to stop automation – even doctors are now using robotic surgeries – it is offering alternative options so that anyone who works for a living can truly make a living. The employer and entrepreneur who finds ways – like Costco and others – to pay a just living wage is accumulating true wealth; true wealth is love for others.
>
> You object to a government forcing the entrepreneur to be just, don't you? It should be everyone's choice to make, right?
>
> But you don't object to the government not allowing little kids to work all day long in a factory, do you? How did it harm society when little kids who were being paid little or nothing were stopped from doing so? Didn't it create more automation in the

factories? And is society better off because of the automation, or worse off?

It is clear by looking at the results that automation, in everything from farming to building cars and airplanes has benefited the standard of living of the more modern societies. More people have more true wealth. Right? Which countries have more true wealth – the ones with more modern capabilities – or the third world countries who don't?

You are a good person who tried to teach me when I was being greedy, that being greedy was not in my best interest – and you were right; I was wrong. Thank you for your love.

A couple weeks later, early one morning the following thought came to me, and I sent it to my brother Manuel in an e-mail:

An additional thought came to me this morning, and I will add this to my writing. I want to ask you if that minimum wage worker was our brother Robert, or our sister Miriam, who did not go back to school to get their Electrical Engineering and Masters degrees, respectively, until after more than a decade of working as adults: would you still believe it to be just to pay them less than a living wage for their work?

I want to also ask that executive or owner who might be earning more than 273 times what their average worker makes: Do you see any of the minimum wage workers as your brothers or sisters?

Again, I want for you to reflect on why it is so hard for a rich person to be with God. To be with God you have to choose love, and too many times the attitude that most of the time has made a person rich, greed and selfishness, will also take you away from choosing love. Giving and receiving are two sides of the same coin, love. It is harder for a rich man to be both wise and humble enough to realize what his real blessings are – and to also acknowledge all of his real blessings came from God. That minimum wage worker is loved unconditionally by God – and is your brother or sister!

My brother Manuel answered this e-mail with a long e-mail making some strong true statements, but he did not address the main points of why a just minimum living wage is to the benefit of everyone. I answered him with the following e-mail:

> Manuel,
>
> All your arguments do not address my main point: A minimum wage, or as you are calling it "entry level" wage should be a true minimum living wage. One that allows those who for whatever reason, being lack of ambition or lack of intelligence, but who work for a "living," allowed them to have a roof over their head and food on their table, and that would also allow those who don't have a mommy or daddy to pay for their education, but have enough intelligence, and or ambition, to earn enough money with their job to pay for that education. They should be able to go to school part time, without having to mortgage the rest of their lives to pay for that education.
>
> You also did not address the fact that the overall standard of living is higher for modern countries who use a lot of automation than those who don't. There is a lot more poverty in countries who use very little automation than in countries who do. It is self-evident that if automation created poverty that would not be the case. Would it?
>
> As for what Christ said: "The poor you will always have with you," I would say that "poor" is a relative term. Poor in rich countries with a lot of automation is not not having a roof over your head and food on the table. Rich countries have safety nets for their poor. It is only in countries with very little automation that the poor don't have food on the table and a roof over their head, with no safety net. So we are really talking about the dignity of getting enough of a living wage so you don't have to have charity from anyone to have food on the table and a roof over your head. Big difference, don't you see? It is about the dignity of work!

A day later I sent him the following e-mail on the same subject:

> You are afraid automation will cause there to be less work for workers to do, and therefore society will not need as many workers, correct? The businesses will now not need to hire as many workers, correct?

But Manuel the real effect has been that where a full time job used to be seventy hours of work a week, it is now becoming thirty hours per week. And all of us have more leisure time in the more modern societies, and that is a good thing. Where people used to take few or no vacations, now some of us can take 10 week vacations. Modern societies can now offer funeral leaves. And both mothers and fathers can now be offered parental leave, following the birth of their child. And these are all good consequences, aren't they?

Where it was needed to spend all day doing wash, cooking and cleaning, now with labor- saving machines it only takes two or three hours, with time to check on your child, and maybe play and interact with said child. And again, these are all good things for the more modern societies who have automation.

Only in third world countries in this day and age do most of the mothers, or the fathers of their children need to spend all day working just to survive. And all these are good results, aren't they?

In the more modern societies, the majority have to work less to survive, and only work more out of ambition or desire. And we all know that to have a good life, work and play need to be balanced. But without automation you have to work all day just to survive; there is no choice.

The consequence of automation is a better quality of life for everyone, not just for the few who are rich enough to hire people to do the work for them. Or in the old days, the rich would be able to own slaves, so they could then have leisure time.

So if the result of a minimum wage, adjusted to inflation, will

allows those at the low end, or entry level to make a true living wage, so what? This will mean that some of those workers will not need to have two full time jobs, or accept charity to survive. We needed to have done it yesterday, and not tomorrow.

God wants us to make the choice to love, but it is always our choice; God chose to love us first.

My next to final e-mail to him on the subject was the following:

> The way to make sure a minimum wage, which once set would automatically adjust for inflation, is fair, is to get as many of the stake-holders involved in setting it. Remember what I am proposing is a minimum wage, I would still allow the market to set maximum wage according to market factors.
>
> You would need to get owners, executives, and workers from as many industries as possible, and also from different regions of our country participate in setting it. Again, I am only talking a minimum wage that allows everyone affected to have a roof over their head and food on the table without charity from anyone; that would be the goal in setting it, and once set it would never have to be set again. The minimum wage would adjust to inflation. I would think the higher cost of different regions would be the most fair, since we are talking bare minimum. If living in some areas gives the low paid worker more real income, hey people can always choose to move there. Nobody will force anyone to live in a more expensive area. Again, we are talking bare minimum. No computers or fancy cars. However, if employers in those more expensive areas start to lose good workers, hey we are talking minimum wage, not maximum. Employers in more expensive areas can always pay their worker more, nobody will stop them from doing that either. It will still be a free market don't you see, just one with a bare minimum wage that allows people to have a roof over their head and food on the table without charity from anyone no matter what part of the country they live in.

We don't have this bare minimum wage now, and that needs to change for the benefit of everyone, not just the workers.

Your argument about doing this causing more automation and that being a bad thing, does not hold true. If this was true we would be worse off now than we were one hundred years ago – but we are not.

My final e-mail to my brother on the subject was this one, he had asked me if I cared only about the worker and not the owner of a small business. I sent him what I wrote on giving and receiving and underline the following.

No I don't favor the worker over the owner, I love them both. Please read what I wrote on giving and receiving. Especially the part on not loving one and hurting another. I underlined it.

However, true love has to be inclusive of everyone. If you give or receive, and in so doing your action hurts another person, that is not love; when you hurt someone else, you have excluded God (True Love). God has unconditional love for everyone. When you hurt another person, who is also loved by God, your actions have excluded God from your love.

Many countries honor their workers on a special day; in the U.S. we have "Labor Day." Everyone would truly honor the labor of the workers of the world by making sure all who labor for the benefit of themselves, but also for the benefit of our society in general, are able to earn a true living minimum wage and not have to ever live in poverty; **a true living minimum wage is not only fair, but would benefit the societies which implemented it – in the short run and in the long run.**

I'd like you to think about this: Is it just a coincidence that the more dynamic economies of the world also have less poor and a larger middle class? We seem to see a country's economy become stronger and more dynamic when those

countries improve their economy by having a proportionally smaller poor class and larger middle class – or is it all just a coincidence?

Chapter 7

What I learned from preparing for a pool party and business relationships in general

Life is not always going to go according to what you plan, but it is almost always going to be your choice as to what you make of it. My wife and I planned a big family and friends gathering in June of 2014. Our three sons were going to visit us at our home where they grew up, for maybe the last time, since we would probably be moving from the house within the next couple years. Two of our sons and their wives would be coming from Portland Oregon, and the third from Wellington, New Zealand.

I had made the decision that I was going to paint the inside of our family pool because the plaster had worn off in the twenty some years we had been using the pool. In trying to get things ready for the party in the middle of June, I discovered in early May that a couple of the return pipes in the pool house had cracked due to the very cold winter we had just gone through. I was able to empty the pool without fixing the pipes that had cracked, to go ahead and paint the pool, but I would not be able to run the pool pump to operate the pool, without having those pipes fixed.

Knowing I had several weeks before I would need to fill the pool, because there were going be many man hours of work involved in painting the inside of the pool all by myself, I called the owner of the pool company who had been closing my pool for several years, to come and fix the cracked water pipes. When I called, the owner of the pool company told me it was no problem, he would come the next week and fix them for me. At the end of the following week, when he did not show up, I called him again; "Look Glen," I said to him, "there is no real urgency in fixing those pipes for me, I have at least a couple more weeks, of working on and off to paint my pool, before I will need to start filling it back up with water. However, I do not want to wait until the last minute because it is going to take two to three days to fill the pool with my garden hose, and I have over seventy friends and family coming for a pool party in the middle of June."

Two more weeks went by and the pool company had not showed up, so I called again. I reminded the owner of the pool company, I had this pool party planed and time was now growing short. He told me he would be there by the middle of the next week. And again, he never showed up. I called him one more time. I said to him: "Look Glen if you are too busy with other things, please let me know and I will see if I can get someone else to come fix the cracked pipes for me." Glen, apologized and told me there was no need to call someone else, he would definitely come the following Monday and fix those pipes for me. This was the week before we were to have the pool party, so it was now more urgent. And I could not believe when Glen did not show up that Monday as he had promised me. I asked myself: "why would anyone care so little about someone else, as to make a commitment, and then not keep it?" The truth is that Glen is a good person most of the time, but like many of us wrapped up in his own world, with his own priorities; my priorities just did not rise to the level of importance in his world.

I decided to see if I could fix the cracked pipes myself. I had seen a repair kit anyone could use to wrap up cracked pipes and fix them. In the meantime it got to be two days before the pool party and I went ahead and started filling my pool with a garden hose, hoping it would be full enough by the day of the pool party.

The day of the pool party came, and I had been praying that all would work out, and my prayers were answered when one of the first guests who showed up early was my niece Dannette, her husband Adam, and their young child, Dylan. I told Adam the story regarding the pool guy who never came to fix my cracked pipes, and he told me:

"Let me take a look at those pipes, it is not complicated to fix." After Adam looked at what I had done, we noticed that there was another crack further down the pipe, which I had not fixed, so what I had done would not have worked. We went to the warehouse home store, which is only five minutes from my home, and Adam had me purchase the materials needed to complete the repairs. We came back to my house, and in less than twenty minutes my pipes were fixed liked new.

The pool was not completely full, but it had enough water in it that at the shallow end the small children could use it as a wading pool, and at the deeper end, the older kids could swim. Everyone was having a great time, and all my worries had been taken care of.

The lesson I learned was that even good people can let you down when you need them, never mind those who are consistently not nice, but God will never let you down. God will find others to take up the slack or help you to find inner peace in dealing with all of our problems – if you pray for God's help. And when you are the one who decides to pick up the slack, and become an instrument of God's love, you will receive love from God directly.

There are very few people in my life who radiate so much love in their life as my niece and her husband Adam. Adam comes from a Jewish tradition, and my niece from Roman Catholic, but a more blessed and united with love family is hard to find. They love to give to others and therefore receive much love into their own lives.

I also want to share with you a personal situation with one of my commercial paint contractor clients, which illustrates that when one of the parties in a relationship refuses to reach out to the other, there cannot be a relationship established. In our relationship with God, we are the ones who have to respond to God's love; God's love is unconditional, but God will not force us to love him back.

I had been trying to contact a client who had gotten himself into financial trouble to see if we could try to work out an agreement that might help him get out of the financial hole his company was in. I was calling him almost every day and leaving him messages for him to call me back. I had even stopped by his house three or four times around the time when I had met with him in the past, but with no results. I was not receiving any answers to all my messages. I finally left him a message, that since he would not allow me to communicate with him, I would be requesting my company to assign another sales representative to work with him, because I could only assume that he no longer believed that I was the right person to help his business. The very next day the customer finally called me back to tell me that he had just been very busy, but that he would like for us to continue our business relationship. So it is with God and all of us, except that God will never give up on us, like I was getting ready to do with my client, and that makes it even more of "good news" for us. God wants to help us, but we have to respond with our prayers and with our love for one another to let God know we want Him to be a part of our life.

I want to share with you how I ended my announcement letter to my last employer that I intended to retire from not only my, then current employer, but from the paint industry I had worked for over forty-three years. I believe what I said to my last employer in the paint industry can be applied to anyone who employs people to do work:

We have so much potential in this company and so I hope this company will find a way to celebrate and reward all their employees' effort with no "caps" on the rewards; if you started to do this, employees would never put a "cap" on their effort.

I also hope management will demonstrate they value good sales reps who have demonstrated good sales performance in the past by trying to find ways to help their current company's sales effort and work with them, and not try to put fear into their hearts of getting fired when things are going the wrong way. When you put caps on rewards or when you try to put fear on your good sales reps you will not do anything other than to motivate them to look for other better options.

In conclusion, my father told me the story of a Spanish immigrant that was told there was gold all over the streets of the new world, and when he landed on the new world harbor found a $100 gold coin on the ground. He kicked it into the water saying to himself: "Bah, these gold coins are already starting to bother me." That poor Spanish immigrant never saw another gold coin laying on the ground the rest of his life!

This company's employees should be valued for the rare commodity that they are; you do not want the competition to end up with your gold coins.

I ended my letter of announcing my retirement the way I did because creating a win, win situation works for all human relationships; not only is this important in business relationships, but also in the way we resolve our conflicts.

In addition, about the same time I wrote my letter of resignation I sent them a suggestion for a mission statement to what I thought was kind of a suggestion box, but turned out to be a company-wide e-mail. It is a mission statement that I humbly believed might help to make all organizations better – and if the substance of the statement was adopted – it would thereby make all of our world a much better place. I was talking with my son Marc a couple days after I had sent the mission statement to my company and he happened to tell me how he was going to try to get investors to invest in helping him to make one of his movies; he told me that one thing he thought he would do differently than what most people seem to do, is rather than investing most of the money on equipment, he would make getting the best people for his movie his first priority. I then told him how proud I was to hear that he "gets it" and I had no doubt he was going to be successful. I told him about the mission statement I had just sent to my company. The next day I sent him the following e-mail:

I want to again tell you how proud I was that you "get it" regarding where all organizations should put the higher priority in their investments – the people who make things happen. The following is the mission statement I want to share with you and everyone who "gets it":

> **We believe that for (name of your organization) to always be the best option for everyone who invests in us, we first have to always be the best option for all of our employees. And we (name of your organization) employees know that to continue to be the best option for all (name of your organization) employees, all of us have to commit to never stop trying to always be the best option for our customers. We at (name of your organization) know that by always being the best option for all of our customers, we will then be able to achieve our final goal of being the best option for everyone who invests in us.**

In concluding chapter 7 of my writing I want to say that mankind's history should have taught us by now that not changing the way we relate to each other is no longer an option. We have reached a stage in our ability to destroy each other that should scare us into finding a better way. In the last century we had two World Wars, and it is ironic that the First World War was supposed to be "the war to end all wars"; yet only a few years later we had an even worse World War. We called this Second World War, World War II. We can only hope that there is not a World War III in our future because there is a very good chance that this one war might for sure be the "war to end all wars" because we will have totally destroyed ourselves and our civilization from this earth.

Ask yourself: has animosity and anger ever brought peace in any conflict? I could be wrong, but I cannot think of any instance in history where it did. I can think of many instances where once the physical fighting stopped, getting rid of the animosity and anger brought lasting peace. I can also think of many instances in history where not getting rid of the animosity and anger brought back more wars at a later date.

However, we should feel optimistic because we are learning more about how to get along with each other, even though we need more of a sense of urgency to do better. After World War II, unlike what was done after World War I, some of the victors of that war reached out to the people from the countries they had just defeated, and now those countries are great friends and trade partners of their former enemies. We can see that it worked out much better for both the victors and the defeated when the victors reached out and helped the defeated re-build their countries. It did not work out so well for the Soviet Union who did not put the effort into helping the countries they had defeated, but rather tried to control those countries for their own benefit, and not the benefit of the countries that they had defeated. The Soviet Union's action was not a win, win, proposition, and they were the loser. The other allies' actions toward the countries they had defeated was a win, win, proposition, and everyone involved won. There it is for all of you to see: forgiving those who trespass against you will bring true peace.

But how can you put the lessons you have learned into practice into today's complex world? Some of us believe that others of us are a great Satan who would hurt them physically and morally. **The answer has to be realizing that God loves all of us, not just some of us, and is to all of us a loving father.** Therefore you need to do something different than what you are currently doing, because that is not working. You need to try reaching out to others without anger and distrust. But reach out with actions that demonstrate you want to try to understand why it is that some of us think that what others are doing, is hurting them physically and morally. And you need to let them know you mean them no harm because God is the loving father to all of us – which makes us brothers and sisters. That you truly believe we are all brothers and sisters in God, and that God would want us to get along.

We are all truly his children. Believing that we are all God's children should make us want to please God by getting along and loving each other. All of us need to know that choosing not to love hurts those who choose not to love more; God loves all of us. God wishes we would give each other a break and not do harm to each other. **What parent would not want his sons and daughters to get along and love each other?**

All of us need to become humble and accept that mankind's spiritual journey has only just begun, and then we will realize we need to pray to God our father for help.

Chapter 8

Prayer works for all of us

The most unforgettable car ride of my life.

My third, and most important core message, is that prayer works. We need to pray for one another the more we disagree with each other; it is the message with the most urgency because prayers allow God's unconditional love to connect with us and help us to grow in our spiritual path.

I have highlighted the next paragraph because today, Sunday, July 21, 2013, on the way back from church I received the message that God wanted me to add emphasis to what I had written; all I could do at this point was to follow the very strong message that I was again receiving by highlighting the words and hope that at least some of my brothers and sisters would open up their hearts to this message because all of us have been sent the message from God many times before, and not following his will for us, on earth as it is in heaven, is getting mankind into trouble.

It is important for you to get the message I have highlighted, but it is urgent for all of us whose relationships are in trouble, or for those of us who are working on establishing peace between nations to receive this message. You need to open up your hearts to the fact that it is up to you to choose to love. That it is not God's choice to make, but that praying for God's help in achieving love and understanding will help you to make the right choice to love. Deciding to love is truly in your own best interest. So please forward this_message of love to them, or at least this portion of God's message. Praying for love and peace with those we disagree, is the first step in our journey to achieving peace.

God wants to help all of us. "Ask and it will be given to you," (Matthew 7:7).

I would like to suggest to you that a major problem of human relations is fear that deciding to love another person will make you vulnerable to that other person. And if the other person chooses not to love you back you might come to emotional, and sometimes physical harm. However, by praying for each other when we are having a disagreement, in our prayer for God's help we are acknowledging our fears and asking for God's help to find a way to protect us from harm should either one of us forget it is in our own best interest to love. Your prayers in and of themselves become your choice to love and allows God to help both parties find a way to build a bridge of trust and understanding. It takes hard work, but the pay-off of love and peace is worth doing our best to achieve trust and understanding. God is love, and when we decide to love we are using love as a bridge to connect us to God and to each other.

We need to start what I would like to call a **virtuous cycle as opposed to a vicious cycle.** A virtuous cycle grows more virtuous as people choose to be virtuous toward each other and more love and understanding is achieved. A vicious cycle grows more vicious as people choose to be more vicious and mean toward each other. No love or understanding will ever be achieved until someone steps up and breaks the vicious cycle by choosing to practice their own virtue – regardless of what the other person chooses to do.

What the rest of us can do to alleviate those, not unreasonable fears, is to guarantee to both parties in a conflict, that no matter what other commitments we had previously made to either parties of the conflict, once an agreement has been reached between the aggrieved parties, the rest of us will support only those who keep the agreement, and defend and protect only those who are doing their best to abide by the agreement. "All we are saying is give peace a chance," as we used to sing in the sixties to John Lennon's lyrics.

It is in every one of our best interests to have peace. Peace is a win, win, and wars are lose, lose. Nobody really wins wars because they are such a waste of what is the very best in us. **The rest of us can be instruments of God's peace by letting the parties negotiating a peace agreements know in advance that they better be negotiating in good faith because all the rest of us will enforce the agreement. A peace agreement will supersede any prior bilateral or multilateral agreements we might have with either, or both parties. Peace agreements will hence forth supersede any and all treaties or agreements.**

We need to make it an international law signed and agreed to by all nations that would be stronger than the ban on the use of chemical weapons or nuclear weapons. It is in the best interest of all nations to have peace treaties negotiated in good faith by all the parties who are signing a peace treaty. All parties signing a peace agreement will hence forth do so with the knowledge it will be enforced by all nations – not just the ones signing the agreement.

It is with love and humility that I would like to suggest that the world has now become so interdependent that even the most powerful military countries – like the United States, Russia, and China – would know that if they were to make an agreement of peace with another country, or with a group of international ideologues, they would need to deal in good faith; the peace agreement would be guarantee, not by the other party to the agreement of peace and their allies, but by all of the rest of the world. The military might of every country in the world would now truly be for world peace, and never for greed or ambitions. As time passes and people come to realize we can now count on all of us to do the right things for peace – the military forces of all countries could gradually be diminished – but never completely eliminated because those military forces will in fact now guarantee peace. I would humbly like for all of you to look around at our world and at what mankind has done thus far, and ask yourselves this question: Is this the best that we can do? World peace will allow all the energy and resources currently wasted in wars, and in preparation for wars, to be used for the benefit of all mankind. "All we are saying is give peace a chance." (John Lennon)

You are called by God to stop those who decide not to love and would harm their brothers and sisters from directly harming them, but not to stop loving them for so choosing. God calls on you to choose to love and to do the right things for your own best interest, but not to stand by and do nothing when evil is being done to you or to others. This is why we will not be able to completely eliminate all military forces from the world. Unfortunately, there will always be those who will decide not to love in our world, but we can make large scale wars a thing of the past – so it means stopping them with as little as possible collateral damage to others – or even to the persons who would harm those others. Their deciding not to love does not change that your own best decision is to love them anyway; you deny yourselves the joy you received from giving love, if you decide not to love. God is love, and when you decide to love you are using love as a bridge to connect you to God and to others.

We saw the power of prayer, when back in the 1960's and 1970's many of us, of all religions and faiths, including some of us in the Soviet Union, prayed to God to show the people of the Soviet Union the light of His love, and to do what was really in their own best interest. And enough of them responded to those prayers so that change was possible for their country, which now allows more freedom of religion. It was prayer that proved more powerful than all the atomic weapons we had aimed at each other. But those weapons have not gone away, so all of us need to, step up to the plate, and pray even harder for God to show all of us the light of his love. However, as I said: "at the end of the day it will always be your choice to love others, not God's."

The most unforgettable car ride of my life.

I have also seen the power of prayer in a very life changing personal event that happen with my family on March 15th, 1979. My wife Patty had just started her contractions in the process of delivering our third son Marco, and she asked for me to drive her from where we lived in Annapolis, Maryland to the Washington Hospital Center in Washington D.C.; this is where our doctor was going to be helping with the delivery of our son. Our son was going to be a breach delivery, which was going to need a Cesarean procedure for his delivery. As we were driving on the four lane highway connecting Annapolis, Maryland to Washington D.C., my wife kept telling me how her contractions were coming on at a faster and faster pace. Just as we were approaching the Washington Beltway she yelled out to me to pull over because the baby was coming out. I remember praying: "please God help me, what do I do?" I had just about decided to take her to the closest Hospital I knew about, which was Doctor's Hospital, when an unmarked police car in front of my car turned on the emergency lights to pull over a car that was in front of both of our cars; this car was apparently speeding even more than what I have been doing by that time. I pulled over behind the police cruiser and asked the lady officer for help. She walked up to the driver of the car she had pulled over and told him that today was his lucky day and to go on because she was going to have to handle an emergency. Within five minutes they had traffic stopped on both sides of the highway and an ambulance came to drive Patty to Prince George Hospital, where Patty had a very difficult delivery of our son Marc. By the time they got her to the hospital a Cesarean procedure was no longer an option because our son's feet were starting to come out. Our son had to be put on a respirator, and Patty had to have blood transfusion given to her. Two things I found out afterwards: The residence doctor who happen to be on call when we arrived at the hospital was one of the very best doctors in the hospital, and the hospital that I had first thought to take Patty to, Doctors Hospital, did not have an obstetric unit, and would not have had any doctors with the expertise, or the equipment we needed, to help with the very difficult delivery of our son Marc. God truly answered my prayers at the time of our most need.

I also want to point out to you the "coincidence" that our son Marc is the one who made the film "Moving On" in 2012, and which I found out about later in 2013 after I started to write this book. This is the movie he made that happens to connect so well to the theme of what I am writing.

Today, Sunday, July 28, 2013, as I am in the process of writing this message about the power of prayer, I was in church and listened to the Gospel of Mathew, Chapter 7 Verse 7, on the power of prayer, **"Ask and it shall be given to you, seek and you shall find..."** This is the third of the main messages I am being called to share, which is that prayer works, and that we need to pray for each other the more we disagree with each other to find understanding and love, rather than escalate conflicts. Is it all just a coincidence that as I been writing these thoughts in "God is love, and Hell is not; a message of Love to all," that I have been listening to Gospel messages reinforcing what I was writing, and that as I am in the process in my writing about the power of prayer the Gospel for that Sunday is the very same message as the last of the core messages I am being called to share with my readers?

In addition, I am getting the following message regarding the reading I heard the same day, (Genesis 18: 16-23) in which Abraham is asking God to spare Sodom and Gomorrah from destruction, over and over, starting with fifty, then a smaller amount of righteous people each time, and God agreed each time that he would spare the city from destruction, all the way down to where God agreed that if there were but ten people who were righteous, he would spare the city from destruction. It is with love and humility that I am getting the message of the story was for us to be persistent with each other in praying for our hearts to be open to God's message of love and peace; **that our prayers for each other will be answered if we persist with our prayers for each other, and then if enough of us choose to love, that the world will thereby be spared from destruction.**

It is us, not God, who would destroy ourselves. Just like it is you, not God, who is sending yourselves away from the light of his love into the darkness of hell when you choose not to love. God is

love, and when you decide to love you are using love as a bridge to connect you to God and to others. When that passage was written we were not able to completely destroy ourselves, but we are able to do so now. The message was hard to understand because it was written then, but has more meaning for mankind now than it did then. God is not limited by either time or space. God is, was, and ever will be.

God is always calling you to love because God loves you. Our prayers to God are our response to God which we use to answer his call; by praying you are asking for his blessing and help in allowing the light of his love to shine among us and to guide us in our spiritual journey. When you pray, you are opening the channels of communication with God and thereby allow his love to come to you. God will not force his love on you.

In my religion's faith we pray the following prayer before receiving communion from God: "Lord I am not worthy that you should come under my roof – speak but the word and my soul shall be healed." A better prayer would be, because love is always our choice: Lord I choose to be worthy of you coming under my roof – please help me do better in listening to your words of love, so my soul may be healed.

I have also noticed that my prayers are helping me to feel much more connected with God. It is as if God is standing behind my shoulders as I take a test in school and is just waiting for me to ask, to then be able to provide me with all the answers on how to deal with any and all of my life's problems.

If you pray to be an instrument of God's love you are in effect praying for God to help you be open to God's love; "for it is in giving that we receive, and receiving that we give" (Francis Assisi). If all you do is receive love, you are allowing others to be open to God's love, but keeping yourself from receiving God's love directly. We can receive love without choosing to receive love and allow others to be instruments of God's love. But when giving love, and thereby being open to receive God's love directly, we will always have been the one to make the decision to give love.

It is with love and humility that I would like to suggest that what mankind needs to do to continue to grow spiritually is to be humble and know that the entire ocean is not in our own particular bowl, or anyone else's bowl either. And to also make sure that our particular bowl from that ocean has love as its main ingredient because love truly works for those who decide to give love, and that any principle that does not have love as its main ingredient does not have God in it, because God is love.

I would also like to suggest that what each one of us as individuals needs to do is realize that each one of us has the power to decide to love, which can change our immediate part of the world, and then eventually the whole world. Revenge, resentment, and punishing out of anger rather than love move us away from God, because God is love. There is no dictator or tyrant who can ever take away from us our power to love. And in addition, we also need to realize that God is love, and it is we who create hell for ourselves and others when we decide not to love – not God.

All the many times God has been sending his message of love and peace, God was not sending it to only the homes of those who already loved and had peace in their life, but sending to all the homes, and if that message was refused, then the peace and the love goes right back to any and all individuals who have become the instrument of his love and peace not just to those holding on to one particular bowl; we are all God's children and God wants everyone created in his image, with the ability to choose to love, to choose love and have peace in their home. But our love has to be persistent; we can't give up on any of our brothers and sisters who do not yet understand that love is for their own best interest. The message is not to throw out all the waters from our own particular bowl, but only anything and everything out of our bowl that is not love, because God is love and love works for us right here, and right now, and choosing not to love does not; it does not matter what we believe or don't believe because it is self-evident that love works for those who choose to love. We need not start any new religion, just be humble about our own bowl not holding the entire ocean; God is much bigger than any of our bowls. "**Blessed are the peace makers...**" (Matthew 5:9).

God is great, and God is love; there are too many of us who have been missing, or not understanding God's love is for all; saying "God is great" even as they kill and harm their brothers and sisters in his name.

Is it just a coincidence that Pope Francis' theme for his message in his Installation Mass was **"Every Person Matters?"** This is the very strong message God is sending you through many of his children, and that we have been missing in our understanding of his messages, and not understanding God's messages has been getting mankind into trouble. **Where there is love, there you will find God, and where there is not love, it is not God's choice but yours. You decide, because that is one of the very strong messages I have been getting that it has always been our choice to make, whether we decide to love or not.**

Why is it we do not want to believe God's love is for all of us, with no exceptions? Not believing that God's love is for all of us has been getting mankind into trouble. God is love, and when we decide to love, we are using love as a bridge to connect us to God and to each other. I would humbly like for all of us to look around at our world and at what mankind has done thus far, and ask yourselves this question: Is this the best that we can do? Love is the only asset one has to volunteer to give up. **Please do not give up on the most valued asset any of us can possibly have – love. "It is in giving that we receive, and in receiving that we give**." The power to give love is ours completely, and we will truly receive joy and peace no matters what others do with our gift. What others decide to do in response to our love would be their decision to make.

I have been writing these thoughts about God, not because I believe I know more about the nature of God than anyone else, but because it is self-evident none of us have in our bowls but small portion of the ocean that is the creator of our infinite universe. The one thing I see for sure that does not contradict the nature of what God is all about is that **God is Love, and Hell is not**. **Hell is what we create when we choose not to love. God is love and hell is not, that is God's message of love for all of us that we seem to not understand.**

Chapter 9

I WILL CHOOSE TO LOVE YOU MORE

My sister Marta Locklear passed away on March 14, 2014 and at her funeral reception they showed a video of her grandson, Logan, giving her a sign for her to hang on one of the walls at her house that said: ***I love you more.*** This sign was meant to be given to someone you love and that you know loves you also, but it would truly be in our own best interest if we always decided to do this simple thing with all of our brothers and sisters no matter how much they have decided to love us or not to love us. The times when we feel attacked are when we most need to pray for God's help in responding to someone else decision not to love with love. We can pray for God's help when our brothers and sisters make it hard for us to love them, but "I love you more" is truly for ours, not their, best interest. **"It is in giving that we receive, and in receiving that we give."** (Francis Assisi)

Most cultures have many ways to indicate displeasure with our fellow men, such as the "one finger salute," but only a very few show solidarity, such as the thumbs up, or the thumb and index finger forming an "O" for OK, or the two fingers peace sign for victory. It is wonderful that the peace sign is also the victory sign; without a doubt when we achieve lasting peace is when we have truly achieved victory. I would like to propose a sign that we can use when someone gives us one of the negative signs such as the "one finger salute," or if someone we love say something that is hurtful to us: **we close our fist next to our heart and say to ourselves: "I love you more," andthen open the palm of our hands facing toward the individual as a sign that our closed fist is our heart, and by opening the fist we indicate we are going to keep our hearts open to love; we are not going to allowed their actions to close our heart from love. We are going to demonstrate: "I love you more."** A closed fist has also been used as a sign of power, and by opening the closed fist we demonstrate there is nothing more powerful than being open to love._**However, if both of our hands are free, an even better alternative might also be used: We can hold the left hand – which is closes to our heart – closed into a fist and by our heart saying to ourselves: "I love you more,"and then hold the right hand open facing out toward the other individual.**

I would like to share with my readers what I humbly consider good news. Several days have passed since I wrote the preceding paragraph regarding a way to demonstrate: "I love you more." I have noticed that when I actually did either of the things I am proposing – to show "I love you more" – that by pausing to do this it has brought me a feeling of peace and joy. At those times when I would have otherwise have felt anger or felt defensive toward another person, instead I have felt peace and joy. Doing this simple gesture has helped me stay connected toothers by allowing me to focus on the love God has for all of us; to "I love you more"than I felt I was being loved by those others at that time. It is something I intend to keep doing going forward because I see it will help me stay connected to God and to all my brothers and sisters who are on their own spiritual journey, and that it is in my own best interest. It is cause and effect – if I choose love I bring love and peace into my own heart. **Why not choose love when love is always your own best choice, and it helps you stay connected to God and to others?**

Please consider holding your left hand over your hearts saying to yourselves: "I love you more." And your open right hand facing forward whenever you are praying with others out of love for God and for each other – no matter which religion you belong to, or no particular religion – to demonstrate solidarity with God's love for all of us. Demonstrate "I love you more" for all of your brothers and sisters with no exception or exclusions. Any religion you belong to that would ban the love intentions you have for others – with no exceptions or exclusions – might just as well ban God from their religion. God is truly the essence of love and wants all us to unite together with him in that love. "God's will be done on earth as it is in heaven" (Matthew 6:10).

It has now been several more days since I wrote the preceding "good news" in the above paragraph – and this morning, when I first woke up – it came to me that I should add to what I am saying when I say "I love you more" three Amen, Amen, Amen! Saying the "Amen" would then remind me that I am now deciding to "love them more" and doing God's will for us "on earth as it is in heaven" (Matthew 6:10).

The following happened on Mother's day 2014: I was using the left hand with closed fist over my heart, with my right hand open toward my wife Patty because she was very upset with me – with good reason, by the way – and she told me that I was no saint and should quit doing what I was doing, and that in any case my hand over my heart should be open, not closed, to demonstrate being open to love. The thing that all of us should know is that making the decision to love someone more is not about who is right and who is wrong – it is about making the decision at that moment you are going to love the other person more regardless of who is right or who is wrong. I would like to share with my readers what came to me the next night: First, my wife is one hundred percent right – I am no saint. However, all of us have the power to be a saint. Again, **God does not choose Saints, Saints choose God.** One only has to decide on a moment by moment basis, I want to choose love for my own best interest and so I am going to keep deciding to choose love. I am therefore going to pray a lot for God to help me be consistent with my decision to love. As I have mentioned before in this writing **with anything in life, if you become complacent and think you have it made, you for sure don't!** To be a good person is always a moment by moment choice and that is where we all need to pray for God's help when we find it difficult to do the right things for our own best interest. **Saints do not pray a lot because they are saints – they are saints because they make the decision to love, and then they pray a lot.**

And as for her thoughts regarding that both hands should be open, and that holding the left hand closed over your heart might actually be keeping the heart closed and not open, the following is what came to me: God gave us the power to decide to love – it is what makes us created in God's image – and so the left hand with the closed fist over the heart means **I have the God-given power to decide to love within me**, and then the right hand open toward the other person means **I choose to love you more! Amen, Amen, Amen!**

However, it could be more appropriate to keep both hands open if you are not focusing on your own God-given power to decide to love yourself and the other person, but in praying to God for additional blessings and help in your decisions to love another. **What has been coming to me very strongly is that there is really no right or wrong way to pray and try to connect in a loving way with another, and God – God will always hear the love that is in your prayers and in your heart!** Do not be one of the children at the shore of the ocean that is God and believe only you hold the entire infinite ocean that is God in your bowl. Believing only our bowl holds God's message to all of us has not served mankind well or God.

The Sunday after I wrote the preceding paragraph I heard the Christian Gospel (John 14:1-12) and the following resonated with all of what I have been writing..."**believe because of the works themselves. Amen, Amen, I say to you whoever believes in me will do the works that I do and will do greater ones than these, because I am going to the father."** And then in the church bulletin I read that Sunday the pastor told the following story:

> A young man was getting ready to graduate from college and for many months he had admired a beautiful sports car in a dealer's showroom, and knowing that his father could well afford it, he told him that was all he wanted. As Graduation Day approached, the young man awaited signs that his father had purchased the car. Finally, on the morning of his graduation, his father called him into his private study. His father told him how proud he was to have such a fine son, and told him how much he loved him. He handed his son a beautiful wrapped gift box. Curious, but

somewhat disappointed, the young man opened the box and found a lovely, leather bound Bible, with the young man's name embossed in gold.

Angrily, he raised his voice to his father and said, "With all your money you give me a Bible?" and stormed out of the house, leaving the Bible.

Many years passed and the young man was very successful in business. He had a beautiful home and a wonderful family, but realized his father was very old and thought perhaps he should go to him. He had not seen him since that graduation day. But before he could make arrangements, he received a telegram telling him his father had passed away, and willed all of his possessions to his son. He needed to come home immediately and take care of things.

When he arrived at his father's house, sudden sadness and regret filled his heart.

He began to search through his father's important papers and saw the still new Bible, just as he had left it years ago. With tears, he opened the Bible and began to turn pages.

His father has carefully underlined a verse, Matthew 7:11, "And if ye, being evil, know how to give good gifts to your children, how much more shall your Heavenly Father which is in heaven, give to those who ask Him?"

As he read those words, a car key dropped from the back of the Bible. It had a tag with the dealer's name, the same dealer who had the sports car he had desired. On the tag was the date of his graduation, and the words....**PAID IN FULL.** How many times have we missed God's blessings because they are not packaged as we expected?

The question at the end of the story is one that all of mankind needs to ask: **How many times have we missed God's blessings because**

they are not packaged as we expected? God's message of love has come, and will come in many ways. **In no way should God's love for us ever be limited by our expectations of how the message of his love should get to us.**

Chapter 10

The Sermon on the Mount and *The Parable of the Tenant*

There is only one team in God's team. And in that team the only "I" should be when you say to your brothers and sisters who can make the same decision about you – no matter what they decide – I love you.

Please never give up on yourself and your fellow human beings when it comes to making the choice to love. God, with his unconditional love, will never give up on you. Stop, and feel the power of God's love for you, and then pray for God to help you to be an instrument of God's unconditional love for yourself and for others.

Believing that it is God who will send you to hell, and not your own choices, is giving some the excuse of looking at those who do not follow their own religion as if God's love has given up on those unbelievers, and that therefore those who do not believe as we do, are no longer worthy of being loved by anyone. A very strong message God has been sending to us is that God's love will never give up on any of us. For your own best interest, you need to pray for God's help to also never give up on your own love for yourself and others.

I do not believe God wants us to be a part of the vicious cycle, but the virtuous cycle. We have the power to always decide, it is our God-given right that no one can take from us. We can decide to love others more, no matter what their decision happens to be.

Albert Einstein was correct when he said: "insanity is doing the same things over and over again and expecting different results." We do not want to throw out the baby with the bath water and get rid of all the world's religious beliefs, but all the world's religions need to become humble in that all of our spiritual journeys are just beginning and there is yet much more for all of us to learn. If there was not much for us to learn we would all be doing God's will on earth as it is in heaven. All the world's religions need to ask about each of their beliefs:Does the belief contradict that God's love is for everyone unconditionally? Does this belief call on us to do anything other than a loving act? Does it exclude any of our brothers and sisters? Does it ask us to do anything other than treat others as we would wish to be treated?

The opposite of love is hell, so yes there is a hell; you can see hell right here and right now when people are not catholic with their love as God is with His. (Note: catholic, meaning universal) However, it is not God who sends you there, it is always each of us who have the God-given power to make that choice. When someone does an injustice to you and you are trying to make yourself whole by correcting the injustice, the first thing you might want to consider is whether it was truly an injustice done to you, and then that it might not have been done intentionally. But then if the injustice is truly an injustice and it was done intentionally, it will always be in your best interest to respond in a manner that said: **You may choose to go to hell, but I choose to love you more.**

God is the spring from which all the love in the universe originates, so if there is no love in hell then why would you imagine God, who chose to love us unconditionally when He created us, would choose to send you there? If you were in the worst hell on earth, but yet kept love in your heart – God would be with you – and you would have God's peace and joy within you, regardless of the hell going on around you. I tell a friend of mine all the time, when he gets upset with the way people act toward him: You can't control what other people do, you do not have that power, but you do have all the power to decide how you will act toward others; do not let their bad decision control yours. When you decide to forgive others as you would wish to be forgiven, you will keep peace and love within you.

The belief by the major religions of the world that it is God who sends sinners to hell is continuing to excuse the choice by some of not being loving toward those who do not love them. This belief will allow them to say: "Those evil doers are going to be sent to hell by God anyway, so we are just sending them there a little sooner." Believe in what Dr. Le Shan expresses in his dedication for his book published in 1974: **"To Max Grossman, who taught me that the opposite of 'injustice' is not 'justice,' but 'love.'" Believing God sends evil doers to hell makes religion part of the problem, and not the solution God wants for us.** It has allowed many of the horrible unloving actions committed in God's name to have occurred in the name of religion throughout history and to continue to happen, **and this has to stop because it is not serving mankind's best interest and what God wants for us.** We need to get rid of this extra baggage because religion should be part of the solution and not part of the problems mankind has to deal with; **this extra baggage has not served God's will for us.**

You do not have to take my word for religion, as we practice it, being part of the problem, look at what is going on in our world today and what has been going on for many centuries, in Palestine and Israel, in Iraq, in Iran, and in Syria, just to name a few, but really all over the world. Is religion part of the problem, or is religion part of the answer, as it should be? When Jesus told us **"Let he who is without sin throw the first stone."** (John 8:7) God was speaking to all of us, no matter what we believe or don't believe; believe that message was a message of love from God! **The truth is that he who is without sin would not want to throw the first stone or the last stone at anyone – like Jesus, who was without sin – because "the opposite of injustice is not justice, but love" (Dr. Le Shan).**

Two of the strongest messages I have received since I started praying to be an instrument of God's love was number one that it is the messages of love, not the messengers, which God is sending us that are important for us to understand and believe for our own best interest. And number two, and this one was almost a shout when I received it: **What part of loving all your brothers and sisters is it that we do not understand?**

We know God's message of love is for our own best interest, as individuals who have the God-given power to make the choice to love. You can see that "tit for tat" only works to your own best interest when it is love we are returning and not the vicious act someone does to us. We need to pray, then find the way to protect ourselves and other innocent people, but not stop loving them. You make the virtuous or vicious cycle stronger by your decision – and it is always your decision to make. Your virtue and love grow stronger when you return love and give the other person the chance to love you even more, no matter what decision the other person has already made. You have that God-given power to decide to stop your part of the vicious cycle, and achieve inner peace. And in addition, you give the other person yet another chance to stop his part of the vicious cycle. Or if it was love, you can decide to make the love cycle stronger, and both parties involved will have an even stronger inner peace by their decision to allow God's love into their lives.

A very important thought came to me one night, after having read the book *Unbroken*, the true-life story of survival and redemption of Louis Zamperini as written by Laura Hillenbrand. Just as when it was recorded, Jesus asked for forgiveness for those who were putting him to death on the cross because they did not know what they were doing. However, he was speaking to us, not God; that this is also the case regarding the prayer Jesus taught. When we were taught to pray by Jesus Christ to forgive us our trespasses as we forgive those who trespass against us, it is us who need to do the forgiving. God with unconditional love chose to love us first and forgiveness is part of that unconditional love. It is we who need to learn to forgive other so that we can be better able to forgive ourselves and bring peace and love into our own lives. By our choice of forgiveness for other we will be bringing ourselves closer to God's love by realizing God's unconditional love contains forgiveness for all of us. All we have to do is make the choice to love, and that will always be our own God-given power to make.

In the book *Unbroken* Louis Zamperini brought peace into his own life, when he finally came to forgive the Japanese soldier who had tortured him while he was a prisoner of war during World War II. Louis had a spiritual revelation that **God loves all of us with no exceptions and unconditionally, including those who had tortured him – it was those who had tortured him who rejected God – God's unconditional love never rejects anyone.** Louis came to feel compassion, and not hate for his former torturer, and by so doing brought peace and love into his own life.

The question was asked a long time ago – in human terms – but in the time span of the Universe, only a blink of God's eye: **"Am I my brother's keeper?"** (Genesis 4:9) **The answer God wants us to give – is yes! We should look out for what is best for each other – and then pray for God's help to get it done.**

My brothers and sisters in mankind's spiritual journey, I have been telling my clients – for the forty-four years that I have been in the paint industry: "Please let me know if you have any problems that I might help you with; the only problems I will not be able to help you with for sure are the one you keep to yourself and do not share with me. **I care, and I want to help you."** Too many times mankind has been doing the same thing with God – not praying for God's help and sharing our most difficult problems on how to love one another – and **God wants to help us.** However, **we have to share our problems with God by praying to God. God will_not force us to love one another – it is a choice we each have to make – and then pray for God's help in getting it done.**

On April 13, 2014, Christians throughout the world celebrated Palm Sunday, the start of the Christian "Holy week." All Christians know Palm Sunday was when Christ was exalted as he entered the city of Jerusalem; only to be crucified a short time later by some of the very people who had been exalting him. How fitting to what I am writing in this paper that the day before, April 12, 2014, I went to see the movie "Noah" and was struck by what Noah concluded in the film regarding God's relationship with mankind. At the very end of this movie, after God had destroyed the world with a flood, Noah thought that God wanted him to let mankind die off and only save all of the other animals from his creation. At this point in the movie there was a scene in which Noah held a knife over two new born baby girls who were his grandchildren, and which Noah thought God wanted him to sacrifice so mankind could die off – but he could not do it. Noah said in the scene: "I can't do this, I choose love…"

In the movie Noah came to realize that when he chose love he was choosing God. As I mentioned in the preface of this paper God has sent his message of love to all of us many times and in many places, but somehow too many of us do not fully understand it. God's love is for all us of with no exceptions or exclusions. God is sending his message of love, has sent his message of love, and will continue to send his message of love in different ways and in many places throughout the universe and throughout time. Mankind should know we are not the center of the universe, and become humble about where we are in our spiritual journey so we may continue to grow. We now know that all of mankind has only been around only a fraction of the time span that has gone by since God created our still-hard-for-us-to-understand, infinite universe.

There are many people in our world that do not have much of God's message of love for all of us in their own belief. I have been struggling in my mind as to how we could or should act toward a person such as one who would behead his own brother in the name of religion; I am saying he would behead his own brother because that is the message – if we are to be instruments of God's love that we need to hear: **We are all brothers and sisters and God is our loving father!** Tonight it came to me that what has been getting us into trouble is our struggle to understand and put into practice the message which God has been sending to us: "Forgive them for they do not know what they do." God loves all of us unconditionally, yes even those who do evil things to their brothers and sisters. So it is us not God who needs to forgive – it is me and you who first need to forgive ourselves – then him or her. We need to stop those who do evil actions but never stop loving them. The evil doers of the world might not value you and me, or him and her, as their brothers and sisters, but we must be as "Catholic with our love" as God is, and validate all of our brothers and sisters. You want to make sure whatever action you take to stop vicious actions breaks or minimizes the vicious cycle. He may not see you or me as his brother – but I see him as my brother – I especially see him as my brother because God is the loving father to all, and we should value him regardless of what choice he makes. To him, you and I might be an infidel whom God was going to send to hell anyway, but to me he is my brother who God loves as much as God loves me – completely and unconditionally – so he doesn't have the power to make me stop loving him and keeping myself from being close to our God, only his own choice. Those who do evil unto their brothers and sisters do not yet understand – **God chose to love all of us – not just some of us!** There is only one God, who chose to love all of us unconditionally when we were created, and whether we know it or not that makes all of us brothers and sisters. Too many of us do not yet understand that whatever you do unto the least of your brothers and sisters that you are doing unto God. Hate and aggression toward our brothers and sisters will never bring anyone closer to God who is our loving creator. I am not just an infidel, and he is not just a cancer we need to cut out of this world – **we are all God's children and therefor always brothers and sisters. The fact we are all brothers and sisters will never change by the good or poor choices each of us make which bring us closer or further from our God who is like a loving father or mother to all.**

As I am concluding this chapter, I like to share with you interactions I have had with some of my good friends. One is an e-mail which I sent to my friend who is a hearing aid specialist, and a very devout Christian. He, like a couple of my other good friends who are Christian, is telling me that Jesus and his message are one, and so you have to not only accept God's message, but also the messenger: "It has to be Jesus! It has to be Jesus! Or no matter what other choice you make you will not be able to be with God," they told me. And another example is my interaction with one of my other good friends, who is a Jehovah Witness, who told me: "It has to be Jehovah! It has to be Jehovah! Or no matter what other choice you make you will not be able to be with God." The friend who is a Jehovah Witness invited me to be with him at their national convention held at the Fed EX stadium in 2014. At that convention I was given the following scripture from the Christian Bible to look up, and I found this: Mark 4:1-9 "The Parable of the Seed":

> On another occasion he began to teach beside the lake. Such a huge crowd had gathered around him that he went and sat in a boat on the water, while the crowd remained on the shore nearby. He began to instruct that a great length, by the use of parables, and in the course of his teaching said: "Listen carefully to this. A farmer went out sowing. Some of what he sowed landed on the footpath, where the birds came along and ate it. Some of the seeds landed on rocky ground where it had little soil; it sprouted immediately because the soil had no depth. Then, when the sun rose and scorched it, it began to wither for lack of roots. Again, some landed among thorns, which grew up and chocked it off, and there was no yield of grain. Some seed, finally, landed on good soil and yielded grain that sprang up to produce at a rate of thirty- and sixty- and a hundredfold." Having spoken this parable, he added: **"Let him who has ears to hear me, hear!"**

The following is one of the e-mails I sent to my friend who **is a hearing aid specialist:**

> Dear Mike,
>
> Thank you very much for your prayers and for the sincere love I see you have for God, and that you get it: "that whatever you do for the least of your brothers that you do unto me."
>
> I finished reading the book you gave me, and it made me realize where I will need to do better to communicate the message of love for all, that in my praying to be an instrument of God, I am being called to deliver.

As I mentioned to you before, religion should be part of the solution to all the conflicts we create for ourselves. But can you say that any religion, yes including the Christian religion, has been the solution and not part of the problems?

The following is Jesus Christ words to us: *"The Sermon on the Mount" Chapter 5*

> **I tell you, you must love those who you have learnt to think as you enemies, and if they oppress you, must pray for them. So shall you be like God your Father; you know He makes his sun to shine on bad and good alike, and send his rain upon all men, whether they obey or disobey his will. Supposing that you love only those that love you back, there is no special merit in that, is there? Quite disreputable people rival you there! Or if you are friendly only with people of your own set, that implies nothing more than average good nature; the very heathen are equal to that! No you are to be God's men; your love is to be as catholic as His.**

You and many Christians will say they believe in God's unconditional love, including Bill Rudge (the author of *Who is Jesus?* (The book which he had asked me to read), but yet say we need God's forgiveness and redemption? I am being called to deliver this message: **With God's unconditional love, forgiveness and redemption are a given.** We are the ones who need to forgive ourselves, and then go on to forgive others as we would wish to be forgiven. **He who said: "Let he who is without sin throw the first stone" forgave us our sins when He created us and will never throw any stones at any of us sinners, we do that to ourselves. What part of unconditional love is it that has conditions? There is not a single one of us on this earth who does not have the God-given power to make the right choice – all of us are to "go and sin no more."**

Not truly believing in God's unconditional love for all is what makes religion part of the problems in our world and not part

of the solutions as it should be. It is hard for anyone of us to truly understand love, never mind unconditional love. It is hard to wrap our arms around that kind of love like God is able to do. However, we have to find the way to imagine it because it is real!

The Parable of the Tenants is right on (Matthew 21:33-43). God has been sending us messengers throughout mankind short time in this universe, and it sure looks like God will have to continue to do so. Or can anyone of us say when we look at what mankind is doing say: "We get it, we need to love you, God, and demonstrate that love by being as catholic with our love for all of our brothers and sisters as you are with yours." And so "the property owner" finally had to send his own son to deliver that message! But if we tenants had listened, "the property owner" would not have had to send his own son, now would he? And we are still not listening, so believe me, all who pray to be instruments of God's love are volunteering to be instruments of his love, and God will never give up on any of us; it is just like the father with the prodigal son who never gave up on the son who chose to leave his loving home and celebrated when that son decided to come home to him.

I also sent Mike this e-mail: Mike, what came to me was to say to you or to anyone who says that "**there is only one way to reach God our Father," is that you are right, but that the brand on the label on how to do this, or to the way to do this, does not matter; what matters to God is the substance of the way. When Jesus said: "I am the way and the truth and the life. No one comes to the Father except through me." John 14:6. Jesus was telling us that His teachings were the way, not that He was the only brand on the label to "the way."** When we listen to His message we hear the way. **"Let him who has ears to hear me, hear!"** Mark 4:1-9 *The Parable of the Seed* Jesus taught that the way to love God is to first love God, love yourself, and then love your brothers and sister as you love yourself. **"For whatever you do to the least of your brothers and sisters that you do unto God."** Are any of Jesus' teachings going to answer any of the four questions we should ask about our beliefs with a yes? Jesus' teachings will for sure answer no to all four questions, and are "the way" to reach God. "Does the belief contradict that God's love is for everyone unconditionally?" "Does this belief call on us to do anything other than a loving act?" "Does it exclude any of our brothers and sisters?" "Does it ask us to do anything other than treat others as we would wish to be treated?"

God our father loves all of us unconditionally, and to say that adhering only to the one brand on the label of our belief is what matters to God is missing the message God has been trying to send to us throughout mankind history – **we are all chosen by God and special.** It does not matter what the brand on the label of our set of belief are – Christian, Muslim, Jewish, Buddha, Hindu – or any other brand labels mankind has come up for their set of beliefs. **It is the substance of the important messages God has been sending to mankind that is important. We need to get rid of the "extra luggage."** What is important is to understand each of one of us has the God-given power to decide to love**; it is in our own best interest to make the decision to love!** Deciding to love brings happiness and joy, and will also bring us closer to God.

A day after I sent Mike one of my e-mails my wife asked me to turn on the radio for her so that she could listen to the traffic report, and the station she wanted to listen to had somehow been changed. I heard a person telling his listeners that they were to pray only from the Bible for God to hear their prayers. I am sure this was a good person speaking, but he wanted to limit God to hearing only some of us who pray from the Bible to God? **"Let him who has ears to hear me, hear!"** (Mark 4:9) "**No you are to be God's men; your love is to be as catholic as His.**" (Jesus Christ Sermon on the Mount)

Please, brothers and sisters, we have to try to imagine God's unconditional love for all of us or we will continue to keep God's unconditional love and peace away from us with our trying to limit God to our own small bowl. Does any loving father do anything but love their baby son or daughter when as a toddler he was called "Da, Da?" Or when later the same child called him "Daddy?" Or when later the same child as a teenager called him "Dad?" Or when then as an adult his child called him "Father?" **No! Of course not; what the child called the father mattered only to the child. The love from the father is always constant and will always embrace his child!**

One of the messages I would like everyone to understand, is the importance of what I just presented in the above paragraph. God our Father (and Mother) does not care what you, his child, calls him. It is making the decision to love your brothers and sisters that is important. You can't say you love God our father, and not love all of his children also; just because some of your brothers or sisters want to call your father "Dad," and you call him "Father," or the other way around, will not put the "Father" on your side and not on your brothers and sisters. **No, you are pushing yourself away from God's love when you exclude any of your brothers and sisters who are also loved by God our "Father" unconditionally.** Our love for all our brothers and sisters has to be as catholic as God if we are to truly love our "Father who is in heaven."

I keep reading contradictions about God's love in many spiritual books; when reading a book a friend recommended, *More Than a Carpenter* by Josh McDowell and Sean McDowell, they actually wrote the very same thoughts that had come to me on **page 153: "God doesn't send people to hell; they go because of their own choices." However, on the page before they also wrote: "He is not only a God of love but also a God who is righteous, just, and holy." Somehow, not only the Christian religion, but others as well see God as having unconditional love for all of us, but also having to banish us from heaven if we sin.** Why do we not see the contradiction? What part of unconditional love has conditions? **Josh McDowell and Sean McDowell: "Let him who has ears to hear me, hear!"** (Mark 4:9).

We Christians, seem to be missing God's message of love, and of all of us, we have the least excuse. When we see how Christ is, we believe we see how God is. Christ did not tell us to do justice to our enemies, he asked us to love our enemies. Christians especially should remember

Jesus' words: "it is by your love for one another, that everyone will recognize you as my disciples, if you have love for one another" (John 13:34 – 35). Did Christ ask us to exclude any of our brothers and sisters from our love? Why do some of us believe God would exclude anyone from his love? "It is by your love for one another, that everyone will recognize you as My disciples, if you have love for one another" (John 13:34 – 35) – not by calling yourself Christians! So why would God ask us to do one thing and then do the other, when it comes to love? God is asking all of mankind – and not just those who call themselves Christians – to not only talk the talk of love, but walk the walk of love!

I would like to share with you another interesting "coincidence": In 2013 I wrote the following: **God is love, and when we decide to love we are using love as a bridge to connect us to God and to each other**. In a letter from Fr. John Tizio, published in "The Saint Mary's Moorings" Fall 2014, Fr. Tizio told the following story:

> Once upon a time, two brothers who lived on adjoining farms fell into conflict. It was the first serious rift in their forty years of working together. It began with a small misunderstanding, grew into a major difference, and finally exploded into an exchange of bitter words followed by weeks of silence. One morning there was a knock on John's door. He opened it to find a man with a carpenter's toolbox. "I' m looking for a few days' work," he said. "Perhaps you would have a few small jobs here and there that I could help with?"
>
> "Yes," said the older brother. "I do have a job for you. Look across the creek at that farm. That's my younger brother! Last week, there was a meadow between us, but he took his bulldozer and dug a small river between us. Well I'm going to do him one better. See that pile of old lumber? I want you to build an eight-foot-high fence between us. Then I won't need to see his place or his face anymore." The carpenter said, "Show me the nails and the tools, and I'll do a good job for you."

The older brother had to go to town, so he left for the day. At sunset, when he returned, his eyes opened wide and his jaw dropped. There was no fence there at all. The carpenter had built a bridge that stretched from one side of the river to the other, with handrails and all! And the farmer's younger brother was coming toward them, his hand outstretched. "You're quite the guy," he said, "after all I've said and done." The two brothers met in the middle, and shook each other's hand. They turned to see the carpenter leaving. "No, wait! Stay a few days. I've a lot of other projects for you," said the older brother. "'I'd love to," the carpenter said, "but I have many more bridges to build."

And yet another interesting "coincidence" is the real life story of a "Love Bridge" that exists, and was told to us in the front page article of *The Washington Post* published on January 31, 2015 by Loveday Morris with contribution to the article by Mustafa Salim. It described the idea Ayman Karim had to bring the tradition of the "love lock," which had been going on for years in Europe, to Iraq. It encourage lovers of all ages and background to affix padlocks to a bridge in the Iraqi city of Basra.

In November of 2014, on Ashura day – a day that honors one of Islam's Shiite figures – Imam Hussein – masked gunman took it all down and tossed it all into the water. However, despite the gunman's actions and threats, Karim was planning on starting all back up again by February 14, Valentine's Day. Karim is quoted as saying: "We need to deliver the message that even with this current situation in Iraq, there is love, there is kindness."

I am writing this message, not because I would like to see yet another religion get started, but because **religions and the love for God should be part of the solution to all conflict in this world,** but can anyone say that they are? You who say you are "believers" in God's love and mercy more than any others who are not believers, have to make things right between all of your brothers and sisters, **"No you are to be God's men; your love is to be as catholic as His."**

Any of God's children who reject another is rejecting the creator of that brother or sister. It does not matter what you call yourself to God because God loves all of us unconditionally; what does matter is the choice God wants you to make which is to love others as you love yourself. To be true believers and devoted to God, choose love. People of good will, no matter what their own religious belief, or lack of belief, need to acknowledge we are all brothers and sisters and **add a "Golden bridge" to the symbol that represents their own belief.** You and I need to be part of the solution which builds bridges of love, forgiveness, and understanding whenever we differ with others of God's children. God loves all of us! **What part of loving all your brothers and sisters is it that we do not understand?**

Have you noticed how, when someone is doing us an injustice, or even when we are the ones doing the injustice, we will call the other person, "Round Eye," "Gook," "Slant Eye," "Nigger," "Pale Face," "A Cancer," "Infidel." You call them anything but what they really are – **my brother or my sister** – Don't you? I have noticed that almost everyone we agree with or we know love us are the ones we want to call: "My Brother," "My Sister." **However, God is the Heavenly Father to all, not just the ones who agree with us or choose to love us.** There is not a single one of us on this earth who does not have the God- given power to make the right choice – all of us are to **"go and sin no more"** (John 8:11). And we are all brothers and sisters.

I have no doubt that many others are getting this same message: **"What part or loving all your brothers and sisters is it that we do not understand?"** I am nobody special, or special only in the same way that all of us are special to God's love whether we are saints or sinners. I have mentioned in this message some of the extraordinary things that have happened to me in my life, and my discovery of the "coincidences" of this message also being received by others as I was doing the writing of this message so that you may see the importance of for all of us of the message. We are all brothers and sisters in God's love – whether we are sinners or a saints. You need to believe for your own sake in God's unconditional love, and that every single one of us is a brothers and sisters in that love. However, **it is truly up to each person to open up his or her own heart and decide that love for others is for their own best interest; making the choice to love will bring you joy and happiness by bringing you closer to God. God knows it will not always be easy, but God also will not force anyone to make the right choice so you will need to pray for God's help when it is hard for you to do this.**

As you read this message you might be saying to yourself: "This guy is nuts, writing about love for everyone in the world that is what it is, and it is never going to change." **But you do have all the power to change things and make them better for yourself. You only have to decide to bring happiness, joy and peace into your own life by always choosing love; then to get it done you need to pray a lot for God's help. Praying a lot is what every Saint I have ever heard of does – and you can too!**

In addition, ask yourself this question – **when others make it hard for me to love them – am I adding to the virtuous cycle, or the vicious cycle by my actions in response to their actions? You can only control your decision and actions – not the other guy's. It should be self-evident to all of us that where there is love there is peace, and you are with God!**

I have noticed since I started praying to be an instrument of God's love, much more peace and serenity coming into my own life; where before when someone would attack me I would want to attack them back; I am now starting to feel love and compassion for those who attack me instead. And, my brothers and sisters, my decision to reflect God's love unto those who at the moment are not feeling love toward me is bringing peace and joy unto me regardless of what choice they have made or continue to make. And yes, sometimes when those who were attacking me change their decision to attack me, I can see their decision bringing the same peace and joy unto them. The prayer of St. Francis is put into action "Lord, make me an instrument of thy peace. Where there is hatred, let me sow love. Where there is injury, pardon. Where there is doubt, faith. Where there is despair, hope. Where there is darkness, light, and where there is sadness, joy." **We start the virtuous cycle by our decision to love, and stop the vicious cycle;** God our father is cheering for us! God granted us the liberty to make the choice, but the love choice is the choice God wants us to always make because it will bring us closer to God's unconditional love for each one of us.

On Monday, November 17, 2014 *The Washington Post* front page had an article by Ada Goldman describing how the "Islamic State" beheaded an aid worker from the United States named Abdul-Rahman Kassig. It would seem that acts like what the "Islamic State" and others are doing in our world make it impossible to love them more. If we love them more, as Abdul-Rahman Kassig did, those of our brothers and sisters who do not "get it" are going to behead us or enslave us. Abdul-Rahman Kassig had converted to Islam and went to Syria on a humanitarian mission, and look what happened to him! However, my brothers and sisters, it is exactly those who do not "get it" who need our love and compassion the most. **If you had a brother or a sister who went insane and started to harm others, you would take action to prevent it; but would you stop loving them?** We need to protect ourselves and others of our brothers and sisters from those who do not "get it," but it has to be done without making those who do not "get it" any less of our brothers and sisters. **I will love them more because I know God does not reject them; it is they who are rejecting God.** We have to stop how we have dealt with those who do evil in this world and find the better way God is calling us to find by praying for God's help; God wants to help us. God keeps sending us messengers, to show us a better way. **What we have been doing has not worked very well for us, has it? I have the power to choose love and I will not follow those who do not "get it" away from God. God is love, and Hell is not: If we open our hearts we will feel God's love for all of us – no exceptions or exclusions!**

Another prayer I have started to say quite a bit and actually have now memorized because it is helping me so much to stay the course in becoming a better person is the Serenity Prayer:

"God grant me the Serenity to accept the things I cannot change... the Courage to change the things that I can... and the Wisdom to know the difference." **I want to always contribute to the virtuous cycle, and never the vicious cycle!**

My brother Manuel sent me this e-mail one night which hits the nail right on the head:

"I look at it as the pebble thrown on the pond — an ever expanding circle of good will. Start with the immediate family, next link, and on to all." And earlier on that same day one of my sons sent me an e-mail with this quote he saw on Facebook:

> Before you speak to me about your religion, first show it to me in how you treat other people. Before you tell me how much you love your God, show me how much you love all His children. Before you preach to me about your passion for your faith, teach me about it through your compassion for your neighbors. In the end, I'm not as interested in what you have to tell or sell as in how you choose to live and give.
>
> – Cory Booker, US Senator, New Jersey

We have to stop leaving the wheels of God's messages of love on the side of the road for our own best interest. Listen to the good news: God's love does not reject anyone! Love your brothers and sisters who are rejecting God. Do not believe you are doing God's will when you reject any of your brothers and sisters and exclude them from your love. God's will is for all of us to be an instrument of his love.

"Let him who has ears to hear me, hear!" (Mark 4:9.)

There is one last personal story I want to share with you regarding the power of prayer in all things large and small: I was having a heart procedurecalled "Catheter Ablation" to cure a heart flutter that my doctor discovered, in the fall of 2014, and when I was in the recovery room a lady tech who was at least thirty-five to forty years younger than I am called me "young man" as she was giving me directions on what I was supposed to be doing, and not doing. At the time I did not say anything to her, but it struck me that for someone who is that much younger than another to call the older person "young man" or "young lady" is not very respectful to the older person and somewhat condescending of the younger person to do this, it bothered me just a little. A couple days later after the procedure, when I first woke up, I started thinking back on how I had felt and decided to pray for guidance on how I could best respond in the future if someone who was so much younger than I was called me "young man." I know I am not getting any younger, but it seems that the older a person gets the more amusing it is for some younger people to call the much older person "young man" or "young lady," I told my wife that morning that what was coming to me was to ask: "why do you call me young man?" However, it still did not seem the right thing to do because it sounded somewhat offensive to say this to someone who probably did not mean to offend me, and meant me no harm. Half hour later I am reading my newspaper and there is a man asking one of the advice columnists if it would be alright to say the following when a much younger service person than him called him "young man," because he was now in his seventies and obviously no longer a "young man": "Thank you beautiful (if it was a woman), or Thank you handsome (if it was a man)." The columnist thought it was great, but they might think he was flirting with them. However, it would keep things from giving any offense where no offense was probably intended and keep it light hearted.

I thank God for guiding me to the much better response; that answer was so much better than what I had come out with on my own.

In the larger much more important things in my life I have been praying to be an instrument of God's love. And to my amazement, this message has been part of the response from God to my prayers; **I have never thought I was the best person to be an instrument of God's love, but I was volunteering for it wasn't I?**_However, in no way is God calling on any of us to throw out all the messages from before, or believe that God will not be sending us additional messages in the future. Our spiritual journey is just starting.

Chapter 11

God is Infinite and Unconditional Love

You need to throw all the stones out of any of your bowls that tell you anything which contradicts God's unconditional love for all of us whom he created in his image. Or beliefs that call on us to do anything other than to choose to love others as we love ourselves; it is having those beliefs that have been getting mankind in trouble. God created us with the ability to choose love. Since God created us, we have always had the God-given right to choose love. There has never been any need for atonement, forgiveness, or redemption from God. **There has been a failure on our part to hear – that yes – we have always had the need of atonement, forgiveness, and redemption to others, but it has never been to God.** God chose to love you first. God made you worthy of his love and he loves you unconditionally. **God never created junk!** However, God chose when he created us not to force any one of us to love; **choosing to love is each one of our God-given right to make.**

My brothers and sisters, God's messages of love and peace have always been for all of us and will always be for all of us, never for just some of us. And those of us who believe that "the property owner" (Mark 12) had to finally send his son to gives us the message should know better than the rest who do not believe this, about God's unconditional love for all. **How did Jesus Christ live his life? What was his example?** In John 14:6 "I am the way and the truth, and the life – no one comes to the Father but through me. If you really knew me, you would know my Father also. From this point on you know him; you have seen him." **We Christians should know how God is better than anyone else, but do we? "Let him who has ears to hear me, hear!"** (Mark 4:9).

Yes my brothers and sisters, there are still some who would have you believe that all that is in our infinite universe working so well together is nothing but coincidences. But the more mankind knows about how the universe works the more we know how impossible those coincidences would have to be. And as I wrote this paper I have come to see and come to realize of many "coincidences" that have strengthened my personal belief in the unconditional love of the one God who created all of us, and which my prayers have guided me to share with you.

I would like to ask a very important question for you to consider: What parent would not want all of his or her children to always also love their brothers and sisters as they love them? Our Heavenly Father with his unconditional love for all us wants us to love all our brothers and sisters as much as we possibly can. You can't say you love your Heavenly Father, but will make exceptions with your love for some of your brothers and sisters. If your brother and sister chooses not to love you, always love them more; **they are rejecting God's love, do not go where they are going.** Please reflect on Dr. Le Shan's dedication: "To Max Grossman, who taught me that the opposite of 'injustice' is not 'justice', but 'love'" and that it would not be a contradiction to say that **the opposite of love is not "hate," "injustice," fear, or isolation, but "Hell."** When you choose love, you are choosing God, but when you reject love you are rejecting God. With love you have understanding, you have justice, you have peace, and you have no fear or isolation. **Hell is where you send yourself by choosing to move away from love:**

God is love and Hell is not. The opposite of love is Hell – don't go there!

In addition, please consider that mankind is truly like the child at the shore of an infinite ocean that is God. Our spiritual journey has only just begun. One of the things mankind needs to realize is that we do not have to fill any of our bowls with the ocean in the hope of holding the entire ocean in that bowl; we just need to realize that the whole ocean that is God will always be there for us. **All I need to do is pray and God will fill my bowl with all of what I need. You are not trying to reinvent the wheel – you are just trying to put it back on**

the cart so you can have a smoother ride to your final home with God.

God is love, so all men of goodwill need to join together and pray for God's help to open all our hearts so that everyone will come to realize that when we choose love we are choosing the opposite of Hell: When we choose love we are choosing to be with God regardless of what others do.

No matter what you believe – you can't say you will do anything in the name of God – if it is not also in the name of love; God is love! Singer-songwriter Carole King wrote a beautiful song that has to have been inspired by God called "In the Name of Love" because it expresses God's message for all of us:

Do the things you believe in
In the name of love
And know that you aren't alone
We all have doubts and fears

Know throughout every season
You are the name of love
And you'll keep on feeling at home
Throughout the coming years

Change is for certain
That we all know
Each day opening the curtain
On a brand new show

Through your sorrow and grieving
Don't forget the name of love
It goes without any end
Forever

Birth and life and death make a circle
We are all part of
To see the light everlasting

Live in the name of love
Forever

A Prayer for World Peace

God help us to believe in your unconditional love for everyone, and please help us to be an instrument of that love.

Where there is injustice, help us to always choose love. Where there is hate, help us to always choose love. Where there is misunderstanding, help us to always choose love. Where there is selfishness, help us to always choose love. And where there is war and conflict, help us to always choose love.

God we know you are unimaginable love and we are praying for your help to never reject you by rejecting love. Amen

I hope you will come to believe in what both Dr. Alexander told us about God in describing his near death experience in his book *Proof of Heaven* and in what I have been writing about how God is – that God is unimaginable love. Well the following is yet another coincidence. In my Church bulletin as I was finishing up writing of this message in January of 2015, the Pastor of my church, Father Tizio, in St. Mary's Parish, Annapolis, Maryland, wrote the following that fits so well to conclude this message of love to all:

> Many Christians include in their New Year's Resolutions to grow in their relationship with God. They resolve to serve God more faithfully, to grow in God's love. What is often lacking in such resolutions is an equal determination to improve our relationship with our neighbors, to grow in our love for others. Today, we are told that love of God and love of neighbor are two side of the same coin. We cannot have the one without the other also.
>
> Today, the Church celebrates the Feast of the Baptism of the Lord. You know, we celebrate birthdays with a lot of fuss: but never our baptism. How many of you know the date of your Baptism? I don't. And if I had to guess, I am not sure many of you

do either, except for our newly baptized of course. Yet, this is our birthday as Christians! By our baptism into Christ we became sons and daughters of a large family, the family of God. From that moment on, God became our Father in a special way, and all other children of God became our brothers and sisters. Each time we say that special prayer of God's children, the Our Father, we are in effect saying that God's children everywhere are our brothers and sisters.

How many of you remember the movie, *The Blues Brothers*, with John Belushi and Dan Ackroyd? In the movie they repeat their famous line, "We're on a mission from God." Well, with proper qualifications, Jesus could have said something very similar on the day He was baptized: "I'm on a mission from my Heavenly Father, and the mission officially begins now – at this moment! "

Because of our Baptism, we too, you and I, have a mission also; to continue the work of Jesus, by loving God and our neighbor. With God's grace and help, this is **Not** mission impossible! Accept the challenge, live the resolution, fulfill the mission!

I respectfully want to tell you that Baptism or any other initiation into a set of belief is **a symbol of a commitment to God by you, and very important to you. But not the substance of the commitment. It is important to you – because it is important for you to commit to love God and therefore commit to love each other. It is only important to God because of God's love for us! Jesus Christ was on "a mission from God" from the day he was conceived, and so are WE!** However, your "mission from God" is not going to be "mission impossible" if you pray a lot in making your moment by moment decision to love. God is love, and Hell is not. God loves saintly Father Tizio unconditionally. But God also loves the evil doer who chop off his brother's head unconditionally. It is saintly Father Tizio who is choosing to love God, and the evil doer who chop off his brother's head who rejects God! **"You didn't choose me. I chose you. I appointed you so that you might go and produce lasting fruit,**

so that the Father will give you whatever you ask for, using my name." (John 15:16) And that belief, "using my name," would have to go! **Unless you believe from your heart that "using my name" means any of the many names people of all faiths call God.** It would contradict the idea that God's love is for everyone unconditionally – you would be believing there is a condition when you pray – if you have to use a particular name when you pray to God or you might not get whatever you ask for. **It would be as if a father said to his baby son who is just learning to talk: "you can't call me Da, Da – you have to call me father – if you want me to answer your prayers?"** All of mankind is still in Spiritual Nursery School. Why do you think otherwise? What part of loving all your brothers and sisters is it that you don't understand? **Would spiritually mature adults solve their differences by killing each other?** Should we have found a better way by now? God has guided me to give it to you again because you may have refused to hear him: It is **the substance of the way.** God chose to love you first – including the evil doers of the world – it is they who do evil who reject God! **"No you are to be God's men; your love is to be as catholic as His."** (Jesus Christ Sermon on the Mount) **For the Power and the Glory is God (Love).**

Chapter 12

Conclusion: The Substance of the Way to be with God is to Choose Love

A friend, whom I have known for over thirty-five years, and who was born in the middle-east, Lebanon, sent me this e-mail joke that had been forwarded to him that was funny, but only because it plays on the words of the Lord's prayer and the brands that were sponsoring the Lord's prayer, as being what is important, and not the substance of the prayer:

Now we know . . . .

> The people at Starbucks managed to arrange a meeting with the Pope at the Vatican.
>
> After receiving the papal blessing, the Starbucks official whispers,
>
> "Your Eminence, we have an offer for you. Starbucks is prepared to donate $100 million a year to the church if you change the Lord's Prayer from 'give us this day our daily bread' to 'give us this day our daily coffee.'"
>
> The Pope responds, "That is impossible. The prayer is the word of the Lord. It must not be changed."
>
> "Well," says the Starbucks man, "we anticipated your reluctance. For this reason we will increase our offer to $300 million."
>
> "My son, it is impossible. For the prayer is the word of the Lord, and it must not be changed."
>
> The Starbucks guy says, "Your Holiness, we at Starbucks respect your adherence to the faith, but we do have one final offer...
>
> We will donate $500 million a year – that's half a billion dollars

– to the great Catholic Church if you would only change the Lord's Prayer from 'give us this day our daily bread' to 'give us this day our daily coffee.'

"Please consider it." And he leaves.

The next day the Pope convenes the College of Cardinals.

"There is some good news," he announces, "and some bad news.

The good news is that the Church will come into $500 million."

"And the bad news, your Holiness?" asks a Cardinal.

"We're losing the Wonder Bread account."

I had been praying – specifically – for some way to illustrate and make it clear to you how God does not care about the brands, or who is sponsoring his messages, but only the substance of the way to be to be closer to Him. God had my friend who was born in the middle-east send me the above joke. The joke that is funny, but only because it should be self-evident to all of us that it is the substance of God's messages that is important – and not the brands sponsoring any-and-all of his messages of love.

And it was only the day after, Easter Sunday, March 28, 2016, that it was revealed to me when I first woke up – the Monday also known as "Bright Monday" or "Renewal Monday" that the above joke sent to me by my middle-eastern-born-friend starts with *Now we know…*

We Christians seem to be missing that Christ being the son of God is important, but not the substance of what was, and is **urgent.** The parable of the Tenants, Mark 12, gives you the answer. The landlord kept sending his servants to the tenants, and when they continued to ignore his message he finally sent his son to affirm to the tenants the importance of the message. **The son being sent by the landlord to the tenants was to illustrate and affirm the importance to the landlord of the message to the tenants, not the importance of the**

landlord's son. What is both urgent and important is what Christ told us in his Sermon on the Mount. You are to pay attention and love the messages from God first; you can't say you love the messenger and then disregard the messages.

'An angel was speaking to him.' Jesus answered, 'That voice did not come for my sake, but for yours."(John 12:29)

However, it is by no mean only Christians who believe that atheists and agnostics are somehow not unconditionally loved by God, and will spend their eternal life in hell, no matter how they live their lives. I mentioned to you earlier in this writing that **atheists and agnostics who see everyone in the world as their brothers and sisters, with no exceptions, get the substance of the message of love God has been trying to send us – and God will welcome them into our home with God – because God is love. When you choose love you are choosing God, whether you know it or not. The first step is always to realize that God is love, and when you decide to love you are using love as a bridge to connect you to God and others.** However, knowing it, just gives you less of an excuse than if you don't know it, and the more that you will need to atone to others who you chose not to love. Not knowing it makes it harder for those – who because of their belief – are not able to ask for help from their Heavenly Father. "**Ask and it shall be given you**" (Matthew 7:7) **is the important part that the atheists and agnostics who love all of their brothers and sisters are missing.**

I want to share with you another instance of the power of prayer. On the weekend of March 22, 2015, when I was praying for guidance as to when, and what I should do in trying to get this message published, the following was the Gospel read at the Sunday mass celebrated by Father Costello and the homily he gave us, after the reading at St. Mary's Roman Catholic Church in Annapolis: The Gospel was John 12:20-33, **"When the crowd of bystanders heard the voice, they said it was thunder. Others maintained, 'An angel was speaking to him.' Jesus answered, 'That voice did not come for my sake, but for yours."**

(John 12:29) Father Costello in his homily then asked us to think about what questions we would want to ask God if we could be in front of God and had the opportunity to ask anything we wanted to ask. And I thought about what the Gospel reading had just said Jesus told us about the voice from heaven, **"That voice did not come for my sake, but for yours"** (John 12:29). And there I was praying for guidance as to when, and what I should do to publish this writing, the writing in which I am being guided to tell you to ask four simple questions about any of your beliefs to see if they came from God, and that it is the message that is important, not the messenger: **Does the belief contradict that God's love is for everyone unconditionally? Does this belief call on us to do anything other than a loving act? Does it exclude any of our brothers and sisters? Does it ask us to do anything other than treat others as we would wish to be treated?**

So we need to accept that the two brothers from the Boston terrorist attack and the two brothers from the Paris terrorist attack are also our brothers in God's love. It was they who rejected God by not understanding we are all brothers and sisters from the moment we are conceived because **God is our loving father with no exceptions or exclusions no matter what we do or don't do!**

One of the things many of us are missing – and is getting many of us to take actions that are not loving – is this concept that any one of us have to atone to God for what we do, or what others do to be closer to God. But no, there is no atonement to God ever needed, only to each other. When you atone to someone you have harmed – intentionally or unintentionally – you make it easier for both of you to have a more loving relationship. However, **our relationship with God has unconditional and unimaginable love for us from God's part – so no atonement is ever needed. Only to go and sin no more. And the last part – to go and sin no more is for your own best interest – not God's.** The son in the prodigal son story only hurt his Father because of his Father's love for him. When the son finally realized how his decision to move away from his Father was making him miserable – he came back Home – and the Father celebrated and was happy for him because of the love the Father had for the son. (Luke 15:11-32) **Deciding to love brings you closer to God because God is love – and Hell is not!**

I want you to think about this: One of the most Saintly persons I know, Father Tizio, told us that it was: "By our baptism into Christ we became sons and daughters of a large family, the family of God. From that moment on, God became our Father in a special way, and all other children of God became our brothers and sisters." A virtuous and righteous person like Father Tizio is telling us we only become sons and daughters of the family of God from the moment of our baptism, and not from the moment of our conception. **Think about it!**

Why is religion part of the problem and not part of the solution? When does God start loving you and when does God stop loving you? Most of us don't get it; we need to love you God and demonstrate that love by being as catholic with our love for all of our brothers and sisters as you are with yours. God's love is unconditional, AND for all of us – NOT just some of us.

"Let him who has ears to hear me, hear!" (Mark 4:9)

"So shall you be like God your Father; you know He makes his sun to shine on bad and good alike, and send his rain upon all men, whether they obey or disobey his will." And: "No you are to be God's men; your love is to be as catholic as His." Jesus Christ Sermon on the Mount

What chance that four brothers, the two from the Boston terrorist attack, and the two from the Paris terrorist attack, would see us as their brothers? We know they did not lead the most virtuous life. How could they see the real truth God has been sending his messengers throughout history to tell us? Virtuous and righteous people like Father Tizio do not seem to – if we judge their belief by what they tell us. God is our loving father with no exceptions or exclusions – and that makes us all very special indeed; we are all special in the eyes of God our Father from the day we are conceived regardless of anything we do, or don't do. God never rejects any one of us, it is always we who reject God when we do not choose love.

All of us are God's children – and therefore brothers and sisters – from the moment we are conceived and it is by **the substance of your choice and commitment to do God's will, on earth at it is in Heaven,** that you grow closer to God or move away from God.

Do not choose love out of fear of punishment that if you don't love, God will punish you; you will be doing that to yourself. By your decisions not to love, you will be moving away from the light of God's love into the darkness of Hell where there is no love. "The opposite of injustice is not justice, but love." (Dr. LeShan) **You are to choose love because: "Birth and life and death make a circle – We are all part of – To see the light everlasting – Live in the name of love – Forever" (Carole King)**

Father Tizio was correct and right on when he told us in the church's bulletin, that: **"love of God and love of neighbor are two side of the same coin." So my brothers and sisters you can't do one and not do the other because God is our loving Father and never excludes any of our brothers and sisters from His love.**

All of us will continue to have all the chances in the world; God is indeed great! God's love for us is totally unconditional. God will always love you no matter what you do or don't do! Do not reject God's love by rejecting to love any of your brothers and sisters – do not follow them where they are going if they are rejecting God's love.

I am on a mission from God, but one of the most important parts of the message that I am being called to deliver is: So are you! All the messages from God will never self-destruct – you have the God-given right to reject the mission God assigned you from the day you were conceived – but the really good news is that God's love will never give up on anyone of us.

I want to conclude with yet one more interesting "coincidence": On a Friday, February 12, 2016 (reported in the Washington Post) the two leaders of two major Christian churches, Pope Francis and Patriarch Kirill I, met for the first time since the Great Schism of 1054 over papal authority and other disputes, which split the Roman Catholic and Greek Orthodox Christian churches. They met to speak to each other about Christian unity. They happened to meet in Habana, Cuba, the same country, and the same city in which the incident with the bicycle bully and my father happened back in 1959. The incident illustrating what God our father is not: "God is on my side, not the other guy's." However, God is the father to all of us – not just Christians, or Muslims, or any other religious beliefs – and he loves all.

Ask the four questions about any of your beliefs, and if the answer is yes, throw them out – they didn't come from God; those beliefs have made any of our religions which hold on to those beliefs part of the problem, and not the loving solutions God wants for us. How do any of the beliefs that answers yes to any and all of the questions serving mankind well? How are they doing God's will on earth as it is in Heaven? We need to ask the four questions about any of our religion's beliefs – no matter how long those beliefs have been held – and where they have been written: **Does the belief contradict that God's love is for everyone unconditionally? Does this belief call on us to do anything other than a loving act? Does it exclude any of our brothers and sisters? Does it ask us to do anything other than treat others as we would wish to be treated?**

The two Christian leaders called each other brothers when they were leaving their meeting in Habana, Cuba – after almost a thousand years of not talking to each other. At the time, they forgot to show what was most important about the way of what Christ told us.

Those "very heathen," Christ mentioned in his Sermon on The Mount, with which the two leaders were concerned in their meeting, who don't understand Christ's way, are the ones who really need to be showed the most – by our love – that we are all brothers and sisters; God is the father to all of us with no exceptions or exclusions. We have to pray – and then find the way to protect ourselves and all innocent people from those who don't understand God's will for us on earth as it is in Heaven – but never stop loving them. We are to: **"Forgive them for they know not what they are doing." Jesus Christ said this when he was dying on the cross.**

But a few days after the two religious leader met in Habana, Cuba, however – Pope Francis (reported widely in the news) did say: "**Christians do not build walls, they build bridges**." But unfortunately, there goes another saintly person interpreting God's messages for all of us as to somehow being applicable only to those with the label of what they call themselves, Christians, or whatever religion the saintly person happens to be – but not the substance of the way to be closer to God. However, it is God's will for all of us – not only some of us – that we should absolutely not build walls, we should all build bridges! **God's unconditional love is for all.**

All religions who profess to love God should add a "Golden Bridge" to the symbol of their religions to demonstrate their love for God. God does indeed want all of Mankind to build bridges of love for their brothers and sisters. ***All of us are God's Children – not just some of us.***

Are the children of this world, which we call planet earth, going to have to wait another thousand years before we understand that none of our bowls could possibly hold all the waters of an infinite God's loving messages? So the label of your religion is not what is important. Again – ask the four questions about your beliefs – and if you answer yes to any and all of the questions, then those beliefs didn't come from God. Look for the love in the water of your bowls, and whichever of you whose core beliefs hold the most love will be those who are more of a disciple of God. **"It is by this all men will know you are My disciples, if you have love for one another."** John 13:35. Christian more than anyone else should know: **"If you really know me, you**

will know my Father as well…" John 14:7 **God is Love, and Hell is not.**

On April 24, 2016, the Sunday I had promised the publisher of this book I would review the final edited copy of this book, the following happened, and I believe it happened for a reason. When I went to church the Gospel reading that day, the day I was supposed to review the final edited draft of this book, was John 13: 31-35. This is the one I had just mentioned to you in the above paragraph: Jesus gave us a new commandment and told us how all would know if we were true followers of God. In John 13: 34-35 Jesus said: "I give you a new commandment: By your love for one another. Such as My love has been for you. So must your love be for each other. This is how all will know you for My disciples: your love for one another."

Please believe that the reason the Gospel reading happened to be this particular one, on this particular day, is that the substance of God's messages of love God has been communicating to you is for all, not just for Christians or a select few, but for all. God has unconditional love for all of us – Saints or Sinners, Believers or Non-believers. We are the ones who need to decide to build bridges of love with God by our love for one another.

What part of loving all your brothers and sisters is it that we do not understand? This message also had unimaginable love in it.

It is the substance of God's loving messages that is important.

"Let him who has ears to hear me, hear!" (Mark 4:9)

However, I had to ask my publisher to please add the following event to this book. On May 15, 2016, the Sunday in which Christian celebrate Pentecost, I was invited to attend a reunion being held by the Cubans who had been a part of Pedro Pan. Pedro Pan (Peter Pan in English) was the migration of the thousands of Cuban children sent by their parents to come to the United States in 1961 and 1962 to get away from the Castro communist regime is called, and which had been sponsored by Catholic Charities.

This reunion was hosted in Arlington, VA, by Susana Gomez. I asked Susana Gomez if there had been any particular reason she chose this particular Sunday for the reunion, and she told me, that no, she had just picked that day. The feature speaker was Emilio Cueto, and he gave us a most interesting lecture about his new book on the history of the "Virgin De La Caridad Del Cobre."

When I got home that evening I went on line and played my son Marc's film, "Moving On." I was curious because I realize for the first time there was a striking similarity with the story of the "Virgin De La Caridad Del Cobre," and my sons' movie. The virgin is a statue that was found in 1612 by three Cubans in a small row-boat; the statue of the virgin was found by them, floating out on the ocean with the inscription "Caridad," or charity. At the end of my son's movie a suitcase is found by the girl, who is the main character, floating out in the ocean, and it contained seven small statues of the same lady. The girl then opens the suitcase and dumps all of them onto the sand at the shore of the ocean. She then closes the empty suitcase and walks off into the sunset, "Moving On." I asked my son Marc, a couple days after the Pedro Pan reunion, if he could remember what had lead him to use these identical small status of a lady in his movie, and this is what he told me: "I went to the dollar store looking for something I could use to represent the gifts the girl would leave behind her to be able to 'move on', and the statues of the lady is what they had the most of. It could have just as easy been teddy-bears, if there had been sufficient quantities of that, or anything else, but the small statues of the lady is what they had in the quantities I needed."

Emilio Cueto told us in his lecture how the Cuban freedom-fighter during their war for independence from Spain would carry the statue of their "Virgin" to protect them, and help them. And that the Spaniards would also carry their own "Virgin" to help them, and protect them. But of course, God our father is on all of our sides – not the Cubans or the Spaniards – or just some of us. It is a lesson we sometimes forget, or we just don't want to accept. A Cuban learned that lesson from his father in 1959, and also in 1959 Flannery O'Connor said: "It takes two to love. It takes liberty. It takes the right to reject. If there were no hell, we would be like the animals. No hell, no dignity."

Note: The three Cubans found Cuba's "Virgin" in 1612, and my son's film was made in 2012, four hundred years after that event. And in addition, his father's book with a similar message is being published in 2016.

This was yet another "coincidence" to help you believe you are special. And that almost everyone else who God has used in the past – and will use in the future – to send us his messages of love is not any more special than the least of your brothers and sisters. However, I do believe there was one notable exception to the importance of the messengers God has used – but that was mainly to declare to us the importance of God's messages of love. And in addition to demonstrate to you and me how love is – love is always humble. ***God sent us this very special messenger around two thousand years ago.***

2013 marked the 50th anniversary of Martin Luther King's famous "I have a dream" speech – where he called on all of us to ring the bells of "Freedom and Justice" – and it is with love and humility I want to tell you that I also have a dream, since I started writing these messages of love. I have a dream that all my brothers and sisters in the world will also come to learn what Max Grossman taught Dr. Lawrence Le Shan around the same time Martin Luther King gave us his "I have a dream" speech: That the opposite of injustice will not only be justice, but will also be love. I have a dream all my brothers and sisters will realize the lesson which all of us need to learn – when you choose love you are choosing Freedom and Justice for everyone – and you are also choosing to love God. I have a dream that all my brothers and sisters will finally hear God's message that to love yourself you have to also love all of your brothers and sisters. All will realize that to be God's disciples we have to be part of the virtuous cycle – never the vicious cycle. This writing is yet another call on all of you, my brothers and sisters, to go even further than what Martin Luther King's dreams' called you to do:**Let us all ring the bells of "Love" which God's messages have been calling you to ring throughout all of mankind's history. If you ring the bells of love without excluding anyone from your love there will truly be Freedom and Justice, and there will also be peace on earth and good will towards men. My brothers and sisters we will have achieved the dream Martin Luther King dreamed of, and that Christ died on the cross for. We will walk together holding hands with all of our brothers and sisters in this world and have Love, Freedom, Justice, and Peace. All of mankind will be able to say – regardless of where you were born, race, sex, religion, or sexual orientation what Martin Luther King dreamed for all of us: "Free at last! Free at last. Thank God Almighty, we are free at last!"**

If you did not watch my son's Marc's film, which I also mentioned in the introduction and background to this book, please do so now that you have read what I wrote; **the movie will only take six minutes of your time, but if you keep your ears and your heart open it might change your world.**

I hope you will now be able to see why I believe God is asking you to get rid of the extra baggage of some of your beliefs that are not serving you well, and keep only the beliefs that will bring you closer to God. This is why I am again mentioning the coincidence of my son Marc's movie which he made on the other side of the world without knowledge of what his father was writing. I want you to believe you are special, and so are all your brothers and sisters special to God. This "coincidence" was yet another "coincidence" of the many I encountered while writing "God is Love, and Hell is not; a message of Love to All" Again, the movie will only take six minutes of your time. My son did not mean for his movie to be spiritual because at the time he made the movie he did not believe in God and considered himself agnostic, but yet it fits so well with this writing…

The link to "Moving on":

http://www.youtube.com/watch?v=TAhVJYUx5m4

Mankind's *Spiritual* journey has only just begun – ***Now we know…***

Note: First I want to thank you God, then I would like to thank all who have help me while writing these thoughts. Especially my son Alejandro Kendall Tamargo, who is college graduate with an English major, and a writer who is trying to publish his own book. My sister Carmen Gonzalez, a PhD. Psychologist, who spent several hours reading what I wrote, and gave some very insightful comments and corrections. My sisters, Miriam Schaeffer, who has a master's degree in English and is a beautiful and talented writer, and who spent over six hours helping me with the first seven or eight pages of my message by editing and tightening up of my language and showing me how I might better deliver my message. And my brother Manuel Tamargo, who has double Masters Degrees in System Engineering and Education who questioned much of what I was writing and helped me to better explain myself. Last, but not least I want to thank Joyce Sweeney for her great work, advice, and loving support that went above and beyond the call of her very professional editing work. And I also want to thank Judy Borich, and her husband Bruce for putting the book together so well, and the wonderful front cover illustration from just my description of it.

However, if there are any faults with the quality of the writing in this paper, the fault is entirely mine. The writing is much better than it would have been because of my son Alejandro, my sisters and my brother's help, and Joyce Sweeney, Judy Borich and her husband Bruce. In addition, my wife Patty also helped me tremendously by making suggestions and asking for clarifications of some of what I was writing. She also helped me by telling me from time to time to stay grounded and completely open and humble; writing only with love and humility God's message of love. **This message as well as**

many other messages God has been sending us has to be about the message, and so please avoid focusing on any of the messengers. The messenger, after all, is only attempting to be an instrument of God's love; this is another very strong lesson I am humbly being called to share with all my brothers and sisters.

I would like feedback to what I have written so far, as I have mentioned in this writing, I am well aware that all of us are just starting in our spiritual journey, and there is so much out there for me to learn. I would also like to know in what ways others are hearing God's call to love and their thoughts on what I have written so far.

About the Author

Alejandro O. (Al) Tamargo was born in Havana, Cuba in 1949. He was one of the thousands of Pedro Pan children who were sent to the United States by their parents in the early 1960s, to get away from the Fidel Castro communist regime.

When he was reunited with his parents in 1963, the family moved to the D.C. area in Maryland, where Alejandro Tamargo grew up, went to school, worked, and lived most of his life, after the age of thirteen.

In 1969 he met his wife Patricia A. Tamargo, who was born and raised in Washington D.C., and they were married in 1971. They had the last of three boys in 1979, and two of them are currently living on the west coast, and the youngest is currently living in New Zealand. Patricia and Alejandro will be celebrating their forty-fifth wedding anniversary the summer of 2016.

He worked in the Commercial/ Industrial paint industry, in various sales and management positions for over forty-four years, and just retired from that industry at the end of May, 2015.

Al Tamargo has always been a voracious reader of all kinds of history books since an early age, and has read, for pleasure and knowledge, hundreds of such books. He has also read hundreds of science fiction books, including most of the classics, and many of the modern writers.

He never dreamed when he was a little boy in Cuba that he would one day write a book himself.

If you would like to contact the author regarding this book you can send an email to atamargo5@gmail.com

More information is available at Goldenbridgefoundation.com